Robert Graves has now completed his term of office as Professor of Poetry at Oxford University. His lectures, in turn erudite and witty, are delivered with an authority which always commands respect. The two themes contained in them are fundamental to his thinking as a poet. Of the first, verse-craftsmanship, treated in the 1964 lectures, he says that it can best be learned 'not by imitation but by personal experience in writing . . . and by a gradual discovery of the need . . . to question every word and sound and implication in a poem'. His provocative commentary on certain sacred anthology pieces, and his dramatic action of rewriting some of them with considerable success is lent weight by his unique standing as a poet and critic.

The second theme, which the lectures for 1965 discuss, is the role of the Muse Goddess and the poet's response to her, now and through the ages. Muse poetry, he says, is a 'distillation of love in its most unsocial, unphilosophical, unlegalistic, unliterary sense'. The poet should seek to be himself and to avoid loveless circumstances in the form of routine, functionalism and mech-anarchy which doom his essential independence. The final lecture, originally delivered to Bennett College, New York, is entitled 'The Word "Romantic" ', and is a survey of romantic love from its original concept to the present-day tendency to drown it in a sea of realism. Happily, says the Poet, it may in the future gain favour, if men provide the impetus.

POETIC CRAFT AND PRINCIPLE

POETIC CRAFT AND PRINCIPLE

Lectures and Talks by

ROBERT GRAVES

Late Professor of Poetry at Oxford University

CASSELL · LONDON

CASSELL & COMPANY LTD
35 Red Lion Square, London WC1
MELBOURNE . SYDNEY . TORONTO . CAPE TOWN
JOHANNESBURG . AUCKLAND

Printed in Great Britain by
The Camelot Press Ltd, London and Southampton
F.167

Acknowledgement

Quotations from the *Oxford Book of English Verse* are reproduced by kind permission of the Oxford University Press.

Foreword

My three public lectures as Professor of Poetry delivered at the Oxford Examination Schools in the autumn of 1964 and written with extreme care were too precise for my audience to follow easily, even though I had provided hand-outs of all the texts discussed.

'Schools', though capacious, are not designed for public speaking and their poor acoustics forced on me the embarrassment of a microphone. I must, by the way, have been the only Oxford graduate present without the least nervous antipathy to those gloomy Victorian halls: having somehow, between the year 1913 when I became a Classical Exhibitioner at St John's College and 1925 when I graduated, evaded the ordeal of taking a single written examination in them. So I had visited 'Schools' only once before: in 1921 when I persuaded Professor Sir Walter Raleigh, then head of the English School, to let my friend Vachel Lindsay read his poems there—the greatest moment of his life. At that time Oxford was still so much Oxford that Sir Walter, nominally my English tutor, agreed with me that we should meet at his home in South Hinksey or mine on Boar's Hill as often as possible, but never talk shop.

On the advice of a sagacious Mexican friend I gave my last three lectures in 1965 as conversational talks, not 'sticking strictly to the script' or to any single topic; and watched the audience swell from four hundred to six, to twelve. From which I conclude that the public *lecture*, meaning what one reads from a prepared manuscript, has had its day even at Oxford. On the other hand, I have been obliged to rewrite almost every sentence for publication, simply because no good talk ever makes good silent reading. Yet the structure of these three valedictory talks remains conversational; one cannot have it both ways.

Seven is a better number than six, so I have added a talk given in 1964 to Bennett College in New York State and afterwards polished up for printing in *Life* magazine. My earlier lectures, not all reprinted in full, will be found in *Oxford Addresses on Poetry* 1962 and *Mammon and the Black Goddess* 1965.

R. G.

Deyá, Majorca, Spain
1967

Oxford Chair of Poetry 1964

LECTURE ONE

Lecture One, 1964

Since it is mainly undergraduates, perhaps only half of you from the English School, who come to these lectures, I have been wondering just how far I can count on you to follow my far from academic views on poetry, or even on poetry's homely half-sister verse. How much poetry have you read?

Most of you have, it seems, been exposed at one time or another to Sir Arthur Quiller-Couch's *Oxford Book of English Verse*—first published in 1900, enlarged by him at the outbreak of the Second World War, and not since re-edited, though still in great demand. Hundreds of other anthologies are published in England and America yearly, but the *Oxford Book* remains entrenched as the Establishment's first choice for well-educated men and women. Over half a million copies have, it is claimed, been sold. Arthur Quiller-Couch, originally an Oxonian (Trinity College), went to the Other Place as head of the English School; a gracious action which, enhanced by the popularity of his robust novels, gave him an unimpeachable critical standing.

He prefaced his first edition adroitly with rhetoric:

For this anthology I have tried to range over the whole field of English Verse from the beginning, or from the Thirteenth Century to this closing year of the Nineteenth, and to choose the best. Nor have I sought in these Islands only, but wheresoever the Muse has followed the tongue which, among living tongues, she most delights to honour. To bring home and render so great a spoil compendiously has been my capital difficulty. It is for the reader to judge if I have so managed it as to serve those who already love poetry, and to implant

that love in those young minds not yet initiated. . . .
Care has been taken with the texts. But I have sometimes
thought it consistent with the aim of the book to prefer the
more beautiful to the better attested reading. I have often
excised weak or superfluous stanzas when sure that excision
would improve; and have not hesitated to extract a few
stanzas from a long poem when persuaded that they could stand
alone as a lyric. The apology for such experiments can only lie
in their success: but the risk is one which, in my judgement,
the anthologist ought to take. A few small corrections have
been made, but only when they were quite obvious.

The numbers chosen are either lyrical or epigrammatic.
Indeed I am mistaken if a single epigram included fails to
preserve at least some faint thrill of the emotion through which
it had to pass before the Muse's lips let it fall, with however
exquisite deliberation. But the lyrical spirit is volatile and
notoriously hard to bind with definitions; and seems to grow
wilder with the years. . . .

Having set my heart on choosing the best, I resolved not
to be perturbed if my judgement should often agree with that
of good critics. The best is the best, though a hundred judges
have declared it so; nor had it been any feat to search out and
insert the second-rate merely because it happened to be
recondite.

In 1939, he added a hundred pages of what he calls
'numbers' by recent poets of genius, and wrote:

. . . I shrank, or course, from making the book unwieldy;
but in fact also I felt my judgement insecure amid post-War
poetry. Although I cannot dispute against Time, this is not to
admit a charge of crabbèd age: since it has been my good
fortune to spend the most part of these later years with the
young and to share—even in some measure to encourage—
their zest for experiment. The Muses' house has many man-
sions: their hospitality has outlived many policies of State,
more than a few religions, countless heresies—*tamen usque
recurret Apollo*—and it were profane to misdoubt the Nine
as having forsaken these so long favoured islands. Of experi-

ment I still hold myself fairly competent to judge. But, writing in 1939, I am at a loss what to do with a fashion of morose disparagement; of sneering at things long by catholic consent accounted beautiful; of scorning at 'Man's unconquerable mind' and hanging up (without benefit of laundry) our common humanity as a rag on a clothes line.

The word 'number', by the way, has two meanings. From 1878 onwards, it was used for identifying numbered pieces in a collection of songs, or poems, or in a concert. But as used by Milton, Scott, Pope, Wordsworth and the rest, 'numbers' meant metrical periods. Pope, who himself 'lisped in numbers', rightly disparaged those

> Who must by numbers judge a poet's song;
> And smooth or rough, with them is right or wrong.

Quiller-Couch uses 'number' in lieu of 'poem' to forestall criticism, as he also names his anthology the *Oxford Book of English Verse;* though with the hint that every piece must obey established rules of scansion.

For the sake of convenience I shall use this anthology as a text-book; questioning how far the various 'numbers' included fall short of the natural standards of verse-craftsmanship; and distinguishing occasional poems from non-poems. This is an even more invidious task than compiling an anthology, since one can more easily show what is wrong with a set of verses—as the Classical master blue-pencils faults in grammar, or quantity, or metre, in the Latin verse compositions offered him—than what makes a poem good. I have somewhere compared a real poem to a round tower built of stone, with the blocks so carefully cut and fitted that they leave no least handhold or foothold, and seem all of a piece. Also to a magic circle, from which all temporal irrelevancy has been excluded. A real poem has instant and permanent durability, however impermanent the world in which it first appears;

and indeed however impermanent the emotional crisis which evoked it.

Two pages were missing from our nursery copy of *Alice Through the Looking Glass*, and some fifty years passed before I read them for the first time in a *Lewis Carroll Omnibus*. . . . They struck me as both dull and badly written. Yet reason told me that they were no better and no worse than the rest of the book, to which I had been devoted by long familiarity. So it is with a great many pieces included in the *Oxford Book of English Verse*; if you knew them before your critical judgement had formed, you will forgive me if I ask you to take a closer look at them.

John Hayward, introducing the new *Oxford Book of Nineteenth-Century Verse*, writes sensibly enough:

. . . In so far as the present collection represents within the compass of a single volume the poetic achievement of the 19th century, it does so in the light of taste and critical opinion of a later age. . . . If standards of appreciation were not subject to periodical revision it would contain little, for example, of Blake and Clare, of Meredith and Hardy, and a great deal, for example, of Southey and Campbell, or Mrs Browning and Bailey. What was once acclaimed as poetically valuable is subsequently devalued and rejected. Who now reads *The Curse of Kehama, Gertrude of Wyoming, Aurora Leigh*, or *Festus*?

. . . Of course, many poems in this collection have stood the test of time. Their selection presents little difficulty. But there are also many whose right to a place must depend upon balancing the conflicting claims to representation of poets who appear to have been over-valued in their day and of those who appear to have been undervalued or even, like Darley, scarcely recognized. . . . This gives rise to curious speculation on the influence of the *Zeitgeist*, the nature of poetic sensibility, and the validity of Dr Johnson's dictum that 'by the common sense of readers uncorrupted with literary prejudice must be finally decided all claim to poetical honours.' Why was

6

Wordsworth's *The Prelude* or Bailey's *Festus* a best-seller in Victorian England? And who knows whether the future will not judge *The Testament of Beauty* to have been underrated and Pound's *Cantos* overrated (or *vice versa*) in their time? How much space will the *Oxford Book of Twentieth-Century English Verse* allot a hundred years hence to Dylan Thomas and Betjeman?

Yet Mr Hayward has begged the question whether certain constant principles may exist of which the few dedicated poets of every age become increasingly conscious, and which it is their task to refine. No true poet of my acquaintance would deny this; all of them consider themselves the friends and contemporaries of their equally dedicated predecessors. What standards of verse may commend themselves to the Palgraves and Quiller-Couches—old-clothesmen of literature, rather than poets—of a hundred years hence is a matter of supreme indifference to poets.

Verse is a craft; poetry is a way of life, a vocation or profession. As such it is not operationally organized like the professions of medicine, law, architecture, pedagogy, the Civil Service—all of which, of course, include certain members fanatically devoted to principle. Indeed, though verse has long been used as a vehicle of prophetic or poetic utterance, one may be a poet, in a sense, without ever writing a line. The craft of English Verse can be taught, but no better than that of academic Latin verse: the craftsman, that is to say, chooses a stock theme which he learns to work out with cool intelligence from a memory well-stocked with Classical examples. In poetry, contrariwise, the theme is always new and chooses the poet: allowing him no rest until its demands have been satisfied by lines of ungainsayable originality.

It is perhaps easier to distinguish between a monumental mason and a free sculptor. The monumental mason has learned how to handle a chisel, distinguish different kinds of stone, and carve a few stock emblems: weeping willows, clasped hands, cherubs and the like, as headings for his obituary legends. The sculptor, using a similar chisel, begins where the monumental mason leaves off. But consider what has happened to sculpture in the last generation. Because it became so highly academicized during our Victorian period, which hung over into the Edwardian and the Georgian; and because popular reaction to the profitable war-memorial art was so long delayed; and because the eventual rebels, Henry Moore, Barbara Hepworth, and Reg Butler, won such high-level acclaim that the revolution had to be taken still further— therefore the basic crafts of stone-cutting and casting in bronze are no longer in fashion. The present sculptural trend is to work with an oxyacetylene torch: welding together random dingbats of interestingly corroded metal salved from junkyard or car-cemetery. You can make an analogy here, if you wish, with modernist 'beat' poems, which originated in America as excusable protests against academic neo-Victorianism.

I find the standards of verse-craftsmanship offered by the *Oxford Book of English Verse* deplorably low, compared with those demanded from you undergraduates in, say, mathematics, physics and biology. Real poems have a rhythmic pattern: the variation of emotional intensity from line to line, or stanza to stanza, can be drawn in the air with one's finger. The end usually provides the climax; though sometimes the climax comes earlier, and the end is what the Elizabethans called 'a dying fall'. Occasionally a calm level is sustained throughout, with only minor troughs and valleys. Donne was peculiar in often beginning with his climax, and letting the whole poem die away: like a Lenten sermon preached too long or on too stirring a text. Competent verse must also have a pattern of varying emphasis, skilfully maintained by the rhythmic control of words. Quiller-Couch seems to have been more interested in the 'beauties' of verse, meaning incidental phrases that catch the eye, than in the patterns.

Here, for example, is his version of the *Lyke-Wake Dirge*; which happens to be a real poem, so that what he has done to it cannot easily be pardoned:

A LYKE-WAKE DIRGE

This ae nighte, this ae nighte,
　—Every nighte and alle,
Fire and fleet and candle-lighte,
　And Christe receive thy saule.

When thou from hence away art past,
　—Every nighte and alle,
To Whinny-muir thou com'st at last;
　—And Christe receive thy saule.

If ever thou gavest hosen and shoon,
　—Every nighte and alle,
Sit thee down and put them on;
　And Christe receive thy saule.

If hosen and shoon thou ne'er gav'st nane
　—Every nighte and alle,
The whinnes sall prick thee to the bare bane;
　And Christe receive thy saule.

From Brig o' Dread when thou may'st pass,
　—Every nighte and alle,
To purgatory fire thou com'st at last;
　And Christe receive thy saule.

If ever thou gavest meat and drink,
　—Every nighte and alle,
The fire sall never make thee shrink;
　And Christe receive thy saule.

If meat or drink thou ne'er gav'st nane,
—Every nighte and alle,
The fire will burn thee to the bare bane;
And Christe receive thy saule.

This ae nighte, this ae nighte,
—Every nighte and alle,
Fire and fleet and candle-lighte,
And Christe receive thy saule.

I wonder how much sense you have got from this poem? Quiller-Couch has not even allowed you to realize the soul of the *lyke*, or corpse, is being ritually mourned at a 'wake' with fire, salt and candlelight. He has also fallen into the common error or printing *fleet* instead of 'selte' (salt)—the old-fashioned *s* of *selte* having been mistaken for an *f* by the broadside ballad's printer; and the *l* and first *e* interchanged. Quiller-Couch glosses *fleet* as 'house-room'; a meaning, however, not sustained by the *Oxford English Dictionary*, or any other of standing.

He also leaves out part of the title: *The Cleveland Lyke-Wake Dirge*. This dirge used to be sung over corpses at Cleveland in Yorkshire until the beginning of the eighteenth century. A platter of *selte* was always placed on the corpse's breast to keep away the Devil— as when one throws spilt salt over one's shoulder at table. Three candles were lighted in honour of the Trinity, and as a reminder of three ordeals that the soul must face in its passage-ritual to Paradise. First Whinny-muir, a wide gorse scrub which lay close to Cleveland town:

If hosen or shoon thou ne'er gav'st nane,
The whinnes sall prick thee to the bare bane. . . .

The last ordeal was Purgatory Fire:

If meat or drink thou ne'er gav'st nane,
The fire will burn thee to the bare bane. . . .

But what of the intermediate ordeal, the Brig (or Bridge) o' Dread, which is here merely mentioned but not described? That part of the dirge must be included, as surely as there must be fourteen lines to every sonnet. The omitted verses run:

If ever thou gavest of silver and gold,
  —Every nighte and alle,
At Brig o' Dread thou'lt find foothold,
  And Christe receive thy saule!

If silver or gold thou never gavest nane,
  —Every nighte and alle,
Thou'lt tumble down intil hell's flame,
  And Christe receive thy saule!

*

Anthologists and others have every right to print what version they prefer of an anonymous ballad, or to take the best of a worse version and patch a better one with it. Quiller-Couch has often availed himself of this right, but in his version of *The Queen's Maries*, he has again spoiled the poetic pattern by omitting several essential stanzas, and including others irrelevant to it.

This is how the ballad should, in my judgement, go:

Marie Hamilton's to the kirk gane
  Wi' ribbons on her breast;
The King thought mair o' Marie Hamilton
  Than he listen'd to the priest.

Marie Hamilton's to the kirk gane,
  Wi' gloves upon her hands;

11

The King thought mair o' Marie Hamilton
  Than the Queen and a' her lands.

Now, word's come till the kitchen
  And word's gone to the ha'
That Mary Hamilton gangs wi' child
  To the highest Stewart of a'.

The King's gane to the Abbey close
  And pulled the Abbey tree,
That burden frae her heart to scale—
  But the thing it wad na ne.

Now word's come till the kitchen
  And word's come to the ha'
That Mary Hamilton's brought to bed,
  But the bonny babe's awa'.

O' she's rowed it in a pinerpeg,
  And she's set it on the sea—
'Gae sink or swim ye, bonny babe,
  Ye's get nae mair o' me.'

Mary Hamilton's back to bed,
  And stretchéd on her sheet,
When by there comes the Queen hersel'
  And stands at her bed feet,
Says 'Mary Hamilton, whar's your babe?
  Fu' sair I heard it greet.'

'There's ne'er a babe intil my room
  As little designs to be,
It was but a stitch in my ain fair side
  And sair it troublet me.'

'Rise up, put o' your robes o' black
  Or else your robes o' brown,
For ye maun gang wi' me this morn
  To ride thro' Edinburgh town.'

12

'I will na put on my robes o' black
  Nor yet my robes o' brown
But I'll put on the glistening gold
  To ride thro' Edinburgh town.'

When she rade down the Cannongate
  The Cannongate sae free;
The bailie's wife and the provost's wife
  Cried: 'Och and alas for thee!'

'Why weep ye sae, ye burgess wives,
  Sae sore ye weep for me?
For I am come intil your town
  A rich wedding to see.'

When she clomb up the Tolbooth stair,
  The stair it was so hee
The cork flew off from baith her heels
  And condemned she was to dee.

Then by there came the King himsel',
  Looked up wi' a pitiful ee:
'Come down, come down, Mary Hamilton:
  Tonight thou's dine wi' me.'

'Nay haud your tongue, my sovereign liege,
  Nay let your folly be,
An' ye had a mind to save my life,
  Wad ye sae ha' shaméd me?

'Last nicht your Queen had four Maries,
  The nicht she'll hae but three:
She had Mary Seaton, and Mary Beaton,
  Mary Carmichael and me. . . .

'Come hangman bring me a cup, a cup,
  But and a can o' wine,
That I may drink to my well-wishérs
  And to the days lang syne.

13

'O, here's your health, ye travelling men,
    And ye sailors on the sea,
But let na my father nor mother ken
    The dog's death I must dee.

'For did word come to my father's ha'
    Where brethren I have three,
It's far wad flow the gude red bloud
    The same wad spill for me.

'Yestreen I washéd the Queen's feet
    And bore her to her bed,
This day I've gotten for my reward
    The gallows-tree to tread.

'Cast off, cast off my golden gown,
    But let my pettycoat be,
And tie a napkin about my face
    That the gallows I may nae see.'

Though Quiller-Couch has enlarged this ballad by four verses, he has contrived to omit Mary's bold defiance of the Queen in the matter of the dress; her refusal to be pitied by the burgesses' wives; her satiric mention of the wedding (in Quiller-Couch's version she has been foolishly deceived by the Queen into thinking that they are invited to attend one). Omitted also are the tardy arrival of the King at the Tolbooth, and Mary's proud refusal to be pardoned by him; her turning away to ask the hangman for the can of wine; her desire to be hanged decently, though not in the glistering golden gown— doubtless a gift from the King himself.

I should prefer 'Mary Fleming' to the usual 'Mary Carmichael', for that was the original name, and it scans better; but Mary Hamilton was really Mary Livingston, and it seems a pity to change that too. 'Hamilton' got transferred to this ballad from a similar, but far later,

scandal at the Romanov court in St Petersburg. In the
case of widely dispersed ballads an editor is free to choose
his texts, and it is impossible to tell how much of any
version was part of the original. *The Three Maries* is
such a one. But . . .

If a poet has printed more than one version of his own
poem, an editor again has liberty of choice. Sometimes
the first is preferable. Wordsworth, in old age, usually
spoiled his earlier poems. But when an irrepressible editor
rewrites a poem, as Tottel of *The Miscellany* rewrote
Sir Thomas Wyatt, and as the prison doctor of Northamp-
ton Lunatic Asylum rewrote John Clare, one should
obviously reprint the original.

As long ago as 1927, I protested that Quiller-Couch
used Tottel's miserable, and even unmetrical, revision of
Wyatt's *They Flee From Me, That Sometime Did Me
Seek;* but he unrepentantly reprinted it in 1939 and it is
still there. The original runs:

> It was no dream; for I lay broad awaking:
>   But all is turned, thorough my gentleness,
> Into a strangë fashion of forsaking;
>   And I have leave to go of her goodnéss,
>   And she also to use new-fangleness:
> But since that I so kindly am servéd:
> I would fain know what she hath déservéd?

Tottel changed this to:

> It was no dream; I lay broad waking:
>   But all is turned, thorough my gentleness,
> Into a strangë fashion of forsaking;
>   And I have leave to go, of her goodness;
>   And she also to use new-fangleness.
> But since that I unkindly so am served,
> 'How like you this?'—what hath she now deserved?

15

And though similarly warned, about the same time, by
Edmund Blunden's reprint of Clare's *I Am, But What I
Am Who Cares Or Knows?*, Quiller-Couch persisted in
using the prison doctor's version, as follows:

> I am! yet what I am who cares, or knows?
>   My friends forsake me like a memory lost.
> I am the self-consumer of my woes;
>   They rise and vanish, an oblivious host,
> Shadows of life, whose very soul is lost.
> And yet I am—I live—though I am toss'd
>
> Into the nothingness of scorn and noise,
>   Into the living sea of waking dream,
> Where there is neither sense of life, nor joys,
>   But the huge shipwreck of my own esteem
> And all that's dear. Even those I loved the best
> Are strange—nay, they are stranger than the rest.
>
> I long for scenes where man has never trod—
>   For scenes where woman never smiled or wept—
> There to abide with my Creator, God,
>   And sleep as I in childhood sweetly slept,
> Full of high thoughts, unborn. So let me lie—
> The grass below; above, the vaulted sky.

The original was:

> I am: yet what I am none cares or knows,
>   My friends forsake me like a memory lost;
> I am the self-consumer of my woes,
>   They rise and vanish in oblivious host,
> Like shades in love and death's oblivion lost;
> And yet I am, and live with shadows tost
>
> Into the nothingness of scorn and noise,
>   Into the living sea of waking dreams,

16

Where there is neither sense of life nor joys,
But the vast shipwreck of my life's esteems;
And e'en the dearest—that I loved the best—
Are strange—nay, rather stranger than the rest.

I long for scenes where man has never trod,
A place where woman never smiled nor wept;
There to abide with my Creator, God,
And sleep as I in childhood sweetly slept:
Untroubling and untroubled where I lie,
The grass below—above, the vaulted sky.

The hero of the *Oxford Book of English Verse* is Matthew Arnold, my predecessor in this Chair exactly a century ago, and venerated by Quiller-Couch. Arnold won the poetry prize at Rugby School with a well-written number, *Alaric at Rome;* and the Newdigate Prize here at Oxford with an equally competent *Cromwell.* He was so capable, honest and humourless a monumental mason that he deserves more honour than most of his energetic and vainglorious contemporaries— the Brownings, Tennysons and Rossettis. Here are three very well-managed stanzas of his from *The Scholar-Gipsy:*

Go, for they call you, Shepherd, from the hill;
Go, Shepherd, and untie the wattled cotes;
No longer leave the wistful flock unfed,
Nor let thy bawling fellows rack their throats,
Nor the cropp'd grasses shoot another head.
But when the fields are still,
And the tired men and dogs all gone to rest,
And only the white sheep are sometimes seen
Cross and recross the strips of moon-blanch'd green;
Come, Shepherd, and again begin the quest. . . .

O born in days when wits were fresh and clear,
And life ran gaily as the sparkling Thames;

17

Before this strange disease of modern life,
With its sick hurry, its divided aims,
Its heads o'er tax'd, its palsied hearts, was rife—
Fly hence, our contact fear!
Still fly, plunge deeper in the bowering wood!
Averse, as Dido did with gesture stern
From her false friend's approach in Hades turn,
Wave us away, and keep thy solitude.

Still nursing the unconquerable hope,
Still clutching the inviolable shade,
With a free onward impulse brushing through,
By night, the silver'd branches of the glade—
Far on the forest-skirts, where none pursue,
On some mild pastoral slope
Emerge, and resting on the moonlit pales,
Freshen thy flowers, as in former years,
With dew, or listen with enchanted ears,
From the dark dingles, to the nightingales. . . .

But for whom are poems like this written? They belong to an old, old realm of poetic artificiality which starts with Virgil's mannered Latin borrowings from the Greek *Idylls* of Theocritus who, though an Alexandrian, had a genuine feeling for the Sicilian countryside; and continues with mannered Italian borrowings from Virgil by the fifteenth-century Italian Baptista Mantuanus, and from Mantuanus by Sannazaro the Neopolitan; and further English borrowings from Sannazaro by the Elizabethan University wits—Greene, Peele, Lodge, Sidney—and by Spenser in his *Shepheards Calendar*. Shakespeare, indeed, who missed a University education, satirized the Arcadian pastoral in his *Love's Labour's Lost*, contrasting the false countryfolk with the true. Milton capitulated to it, though he followed Spenser's example in lending the scene English trees and flowers. The tradition is an insincere pretence of the dilettante city man that he wishes himself a simple yokel; and the construction of a pasteboard theatre for Arcadian dreams of lost poetic truth.

Readers accept the imposture, out of politeness to the schoolmasters who descant on its Classical beauty and who judge each new pastoral piece solely by its tunefulness and correctness. Matthew Arnold, the last capable performer in this style, was more sincere than most of his predecessors. Though continuously engrossed with his post as Inspector of Schools for the Board of Education, he hankered for the countryside:

> Too rare, too rare, grow now my visits here!
>> But once I knew each field, each flower, each stick;
>>> And with the country-folk acquaintance made
>> By barn in threshing-time, by new-built rick.
>>> Here, too, our shepherd pipes we first assay'd.
>>>> Ah me! this many a year
>> My pipe is lost, my shepherd's-holiday!
>>> Needs must I lose them, needs with heavy heart
>>> Into the world and wave of men depart;
>> But Thyrsis of his own will went away.

> It irk'd him to be here, he could not rest.
>> He loved each simple joy the country yields,
>>> He loved his mates; but yet he could not keep
>> For that a shadow lower'd on the fields,
>>> Here with the shepherds and the silly sheep.
>>>> Some life of men unblest
>> He knew, which made him droop, and fill'd his head.
>>> He went; his piping took a troubled sound
>>> Of storms that rage outside our happy ground;
>> He could not wait their passing, he is dead!

Arnold chose his dear companion, A. H. Clough, to represent the Shepherd Thyrsis; and fixed Arcadia in the still unspoiled country around Oxford, where they had

wandered about as undergraduates. Naturally he left out
the Railways, and the Police, and the new Telegraph as
unpoetical; and seldom goofed, as here, by introducing
too modern a note:

But hush! the upland hath a sudden loss
  Of quiet;—Look! adown the dusk hill-side,
    A troop of Oxford hunters going home,
  As in old days, jovial and talking, ride!
    From hunting with the Berkshire hounds they come—
      Quick, let me fly, and cross
  Into yon further field! . . .

The pastoral is now dead. So are Classical references to
amaranth, acanthus, asphodel, and other poetic Greek
flowers that not one reader in a million would recognize
growing—and this is an exaggeration because the amaranth was a wholly unbotanical bloom, and moly is
wrongly described by Homer himself. Conceits are also
out. I haven't seen an old-fashioned Classical conceit
published since at least the reign of Edward VII. The
Oxford Book of English Verse contains some fantastical
nonsensical ones from the early seventeenth century.
Here is one by William Browne, with a misplaced 'only',
banning song-birds and flowers in May because a girl
friend of his died in that month:

    May! Be thou never graced with birds that sing,
        Nor Flora's pride!
    In thee all flowers and roses spring,
        Mine only died.

and another, also by Browne, on the death of the Dowager
Countess of Pembroke:

    Underneath this sable herse
    Lies the subject of all verse:

20

Sidney's sister, Pembroke's mother:
Death, ere thou hast slain another
Fair and learn'd and good as she,
Time shall throw a dart at thee.

In a sillier vein, here is Browne's contemporary, William Strode, writing about Chloris:

I saw fair Chloris walk alone,
When feather'd rain came softly down,
As Jove descending from his Tower
To court her in a silver shower:
The wanton snow flew to her breast,
Like pretty birds into their nest,
But, overcome with whiteness there,
For grief it thaw'd into a tear:
    Thence falling on her garments' hem,
    To deck her, froze into a gem.

The popular view of poetry as beautiful nonsense which has to be interpreted by literary *cognoscenti*, has survived the Classical Age and still haunts the present. American high-school students write to me: 'Dear Professor Graves, we have been asked by our prof to write a thesis on the meaning of your poem [such and such] and are writing to invite your kind assistance . . .' To which I reply: 'It says exactly what it means, and if you can tell me where it stops being comprehensible, I shall be sincerely grateful.' That silences them.

Reaction against the conceit is simplicity reduced to utter vapidity. Samuel Rogers is represented here by a poem called *The Wish:*

Mine be a cot beside the hill;
    A bee-hive's hum shall soothe my ear;
A willowy brook, that turns a mill,
    With many a fall shall linger near.

21

A typical poem of escape; but escape from what? Turn Samuel Rogers up in the encyclopedia, and you will find that his father was a rich banker, but that Samuel, while continuing the business after his father's death, preferred to be known as an art-connoisseur and man of letters, bought works of art cheap in Paris during the French Revolution, wrote for *The Gentleman's Magazine*, published a fragmentary epic about Columbus, became the literary dictator of London, a patron of needy men of letters; was offered but refused the laureateship on the death of Wordsworth (for whom he had obtained the famous sinecure as distributor of stamps). Byron praised Rogers's *Pleasures of Memory* with: 'There is not a vulgar line in the poem,' and he is credited with being the last verse-practitioner who 'could elevate and refine familiar themes in eighteenth-century style by abstract treatment and lofty imagery'. To make any sense of *The Wish*, we should introduce it with some honest introduction of this sort:

My father's business at Cornhill
　Came to me at his death, but I
Devoted more of heart and will
　To the pursuit of poetry.

In gilded parlours of the great
　And rich, my youthful years were spent;
And while I dared not underrate
　Such luscious comfort as they lent,

Often I wished myself obscure,
　A simple-minded country clown
With healthful frame and morals pure,
　And thus I wrote these wishes down:

*

22

Mine be a cot beside the hill;
  A bee-hive's hum shall soothe my ear;
A willowy brook, that turns a mill,
  With many a fall shall linger near.

The swallow oft beneath my thatch
  Shall twitter from her clay-built nest;
Oft shall the pilgrim lift the latch
  And share my meal, a welcome guest.

Around my ivied porch shall spring
  Each fragrant flower that drinks the dew;
And Lucy at her wheel shall sing
  In russet gown and apron blue.

The village church among the trees,
  Where first our marriage vows were given,
With merry peals shall swell the breeze
  And point with taper spire to Heaven.

*

I pointed out four or five years ago that perhaps three
or four million people had read Milton's *L'Allegro*—
reprinted in the *Oxford Book of English Verse*—and that
not a single one had questioned his nonsensical account
of the barn-door cock which strays, not unseen, along the
hedgerows, listening to the noise of the hunt until he
reaches the flaming Eastern skyline:

    . . . While the Cock with lively din,
    Scatters the rear of darkness thin,
    And to the stack, or the Barn dore,
    Stoutly struts his Dames before,
    Oft list'ning how the Hounds and horn
    Chearly rouse the slumbring morn,
    From the side of som Hoar Hill,
    Through the high wood echoing shrill.

Som time walking not unseen
By Hedge-row Elms, on Hillocks green,
Right against the Eastern gate,
Wher the great Sun begins his state,
Rob'd in flames, and Amber Light,
The clouds in thousand Liveries dight.
While the Plowman neer at hand,
Whistles ore the Furrow'd Land,
And the Milkmaid singeth blithe,
And the Mower whets his sithe. . . .

I also pointed out that it had never occurred to anyone that one of Milton's original pages might have been misplaced, and that the passage should run:

While the Cock with lively din,
Scatters the rear of darkness thin,
And to the stack, or the Barn dore,
Stoutly struts his Dames before,
And every Shepherd tells his tale
Under the Hawthorn in the dale . . .

where 'tells his tale' means: 'counts his sheep, to see whether any of them has been stolen during the night'. And that it should continue:

Streit mine eye hath caught new pleasures
Whilst the Lantskip round it measures,
Russet Lawns, and Fallows Gray,
Where the nibling flocks do stray,
Mountains on whose barren brest
The labouring clouds do often rest:
Meadows trim with Daisies pide,
Shallow Brooks, and Rivers wide . . . etc.

The misplaced page fits into the poem later on:

24

And young and old com forth to play
On a Sunshine Holiday,
Till the live-long day-light fail,
Then to the Spicy Nut-brown Ale,
With stories told of many a feat,
How Faery Mab the junkets eat,
She was pincht, and pull'd she sed,
And he by Friar's Lanthorn led
Tells how the drudging Goblin swet,
When in one night, ere glimpse of morn,
His shadowy Flale hath thresh'd the Corn
That ten day-labourers could not end,
Then lies him down the Lubbar Fend,
And stretch'd out all the Chimney's length,
Basks at the fire his hairy strength;
And Crop-full out of dores he flings,
Ere the first Cock his Matin rings,
Oft list'ning how the Hounds and horn
Chearly rouse the slumbring morn,
From the side of som Hoar Hill,
Through the high wood echoing shrill,
Som time walking, not unseen,
By Hedge-row Elms, on Hillocks green,
Right against the Eastern gate,
Wher the great Sun begins his state,
Rob'd in flames, and Amber light,
The clouds in thousand Liveries dight,
While the Plowman neer at hand,
Whistles ore the Furrow'd land,
And the milkmaid singeth blithe,
And the Mower whets his sithe.
Thus don the Tales, to bed they creep,
By whispering Windes soon lull'd asleep. . . .

The original cause of the misplacement may have been
the verbal similarity between *Thus don the Tales, to bed
they creep* and *Every Shepherd tells his tale;* and between
While the Cock with lively din and *Ere the first Cock his*

Matin rings. Milton came to despise his early non-religious work and did not consider *L'Allegro*, published in 1632, to be worthy of reprint even for the sake of amending the textual error. A correspondent who forgot to sign his name, recently reassured me that I was perhaps not unique in my amendment of the text. He wrote:

. . . I possess an edition of Milton's *Minor Poems* with illustrations by the mid-Victorian painter-etcher Samuel Palmer. One of these is entitled 'The Eastern Gate'. It shows the Ploughman at his toil, with eyes turned towards the rising sun while, full in his line of vision, walks the 'Lubber Fiend', looking like a bear on his hind legs, or an Abominable Snowman. This need not be taken to contravene your thesis: that it takes a poet to understand a poem. Palmer was a great student of Milton; but he had also, in his childhood, been well acquainted with William Blake, whose influence on him was a lasting one. Perhaps Blake anticipated you?

I should be proud to think so.

Poetry is the profession of private truth, supported by craftsmanship in the use of words; I prefer not to call it an art, because the art of Classical Verse from the time of Virgil onwards allied itself to the art of Rhetoric, which was a form of hypnotism designed to make a weak legal case seem strong, or a bad one good, or a trivial one important. From the first century B.C. onwards, the art of verse became the art of cozenage, not of truth.

Milton's *Hymn on the Morning of Christ's Nativity* is a perfect example of cozenage:

It was the Winter wilde,
While the Heav'n-born-childe,
    All meanly wrapt in the rude manger lies;
Nature in aw to him

Had doff't her gaudy trim,
  With her great Master so to sympathize:
It was no season then for her
To wanton with the Sun her lusty Paramour.

Only with speeches fair
She woo's the gentle Air
  To hide her guilty front with innocent Snow,
And on her naked shame,
Pollute with sinful blame,
  The Saintly Vail of Maiden white to throw,
Confounded, that her Makers eyes
Should look so neer her foul deformities.

But he her fears to cease,
Sent down the meek-ey'd Peace,
  She crown'd with Olive green, came softly sliding
Down through the turning sphear
His ready Harbinger,
  With Turtle wing the amorous clouds dividing,
And waving wide her mirtle wand,
She strikes a universall Peace through Sea and Land.

No War, or Battails sound
Was heard the World around,
  The idle spear and shield were high up hung;
The hookéd Chariot stood
Unstain'd with hostile blood,
  The Trumpet spake not to the arméd throng,
And Kings sate still with awfull eye,
As if they surely knew their sovran Lord was by. . . .

The conceits are gross and insincere. The Goddess
Nature, instead of continuing to indulge in amorous
frolics with her lover the Sun, puts on a garment of snow
to hide her lascivious body from God's eyes. But God
reassures her by sending down the dove of peace, and
thereupon ensues universal peace throughout the world.

As a good Classical scholar and historian, Milton knew well enough that Jesus was not born in the week following the Winter Solstice (a date chosen by the early Fathers to disguise their celebration, under cover of a popular feast honouring the Unconquered Sun) but probably in August. He knew too that the whole world was not at peace, and that the fifth-century Christian historian Orosius invented the story of Augustus' shutting the doors of Janus' temple in Jesus' honour. Furthermore that, according to the Gospel, Jesus himself declared: 'I have come not to bring peace but a sword!'
Milton continues:

But peacefull was the night
Wherein the Prince of light
   His raign of peace upon the earth began:
The Windes with wonder whist,
Smoothly the waters kist,
   Whispering new joyes to the milde Ocean,
Who now hath quite forgot to rave,
While Birds of Calm sit brooding on the charméd wave.

The Stars with deep amaze
Stand fixt in stedfast gaze,
   Bending one way their pretious influence,
And will not take their flight,
For all the morning light,
   Or Lucifer that often warn'd them thence;
But in their glimmering Orbs did glow,
Untill their Lord himself bespake, and bid them go.

And though the shady gloom
Had given day her room,
   The Sun himself with-held his wonted speed,
And hid his head for shame,
As his inferior flame,
   The new enlightn'd world no more should need;

He saw a greater Sun appear
Than his bright Throne, or burning Axletree could bear.

The first stanza Classically connects the 'halcyon' days
of Mediterranean calm with Jesus's nativity; and, indeed,
the middle of December is usually calm enough; but
when Milton speaks of the stars waiting until the Child
should dismiss them, and of the Sun halting his usual
speed in the Child's honour, we know, and he knows we
know, that this is what Adolf Hitler later called 'a lie of
genius'.

The *Oxford Book of English Verse* contains few real
poems; and, of course, everyone should make his own
private collection of real poems, rather than rely on public
anthologists. But it is a useful museum of fashion. 'How
pretty, how quaint, how vulgar, how neat, how mon-
strous,' we should say as we read.

Before closing, I must venture a view to which I do
not ask you to subscribe, but which has forced itself on
me more and more strongly in the last few years. It is
that both in England and the Commonwealth, and the
United States, standards of verse-craftsmanship *seem* to
have risen appreciably as the result of modern poems
being included in school and college curricula. But is it
not rather that far more attention is now paid to the
standards of verse-craftmanship deduced by academic
critics from certain fashionable modern poets? The rudi-
ments of craftsmanship can be best learned, not by imitation but by personal experience in writing, after varied
acquaintance with poems of different ages and styles;
and by a gradual discovery of the need—which is my
main insistence in these three lectures—to question
every word and sound and implication in a poem either
read or written.

Poetry is another matter altogether. The present trend
in politics, economics and ethics seems wholly inimical to

the appearance of new poets, or the honourable survival
of those who may have already appeared; but this perhaps means that the occasional exception, the poet born
with a light in his head, will be more surely tempered
than before against departure from poetic principle;
which is a simple, obstinate belief in miracle: an asseve-
ration of personal independence against all collective
codifications of thought and behaviour.

LECTURE TWO

Lecture Two, 1964

One of the most popular poems in the *Oxford Book of English Verse*, particularly welcome because it enlivens a long dull stretch between the Restoration poets and the Romantics, is Thomas Gray's *On A Favourite Cat, Drowned In A Tub of Gold Fishes*. It used to be a favourite of mine, too, until I re-read it carefully the other day for the first time in forty years, and realized how scandalously less trouble Gray had taken with it than with, for instance, his *Elegy in a Country Churchyard:*

> 'Twas on a lofty vase's side,
> Where China's gayest art had dyed
>   The azure flowers that blow;
> Demurest of the tabby kind,
> The pensive Selima reclined,
>   Gazed on the lake below.
>
> Her conscious tail her joy declared;
> The fair round face, the snowy beard,
>   The velvet of her paws,
> Her coat, that with the tortoise vies,
> Her ears of jet, and emerald eyes,
>   She saw; and purr'd applause.
>
> Still had she gazed; but 'midst the tide
> Two angel forms were seen to glide,
>   The Genii of the stream:
> Their scaly armour's Tyrian hue
>   Betray'd a golden gleam.
>
> The hapless Nymph with wonder saw:
> A whisker first and then a claw,

With many an ardent wish,
She stretch'd in vain to reach the prize.
What female heart can gold despise?
What Cat's averse to fish?

Presumptuous Maid! with looks intent
Again she stretch'd, again she bent,
   Nor knew the gulf between.
(Malignant Fate sat by, and smiled.)
The slipp'ry verge her feet beguiled,
   She tumbled headlong in.

Eight times emerging from the flood
She mew'd to ev'ry wat'ry god,
   Some speedy aid to send.
No Dolphin came, no Nereid stirr'd:
Nor cruel *Tom*, nor *Susan* heard.
   A Fav'rite has no friend!

From hence, ye Beauties undeceived,
Know, one false step is ne'er retrieved,
   And be with caution bold.
Not all that tempts your wand'ring eyes
And heedless hearts, is lawful prize;
   Nor all that glisters, gold.

The poem began, I surmise, with the lines:

Demurest of the tabby kind,
The pensive Selima reclined,
   Hard by the Gold Fish tub. . . .

But Gray could not find a satisfactory rhyme to *tub* ('rub', 'shrub', 'scrub', 'sillabub'?) and started again, changing the tub to a large decorated Chinese vase, or wine-cooler—an unlikely container for goldfish; one would have expected a glass jar—and making the cat recline on the vase's shoulder. But 'vase's shoulder' would not scan, so he had to use *side:*

> 'Twas on a lofty vase's side,
> Where China's curious art had dyed
>   The gayest flowers that blow,
> Demurest of the tabby kind . . .

He rightly disliked two superlatives—*gayest* and *demurest*—so close to each other, and therefore changed *curious* to *gayest,* and *gayest* to *azure:*

> Where China's gayest art had dyed
>   The azure flowers that blow . . .

though ceramic art does not, of course, dye flowers that blow. Gray either did not notice that, though a poem of this sort demands a constant variation of vowel sounds to lend it richness, he had used the words *China, side, dyed, kind, reclined:* all long *i*'s. Worse, he had not as yet considered the end of the poem, which proved to be a moral warning: 'Young women, never risk your reputation by greed of money or of sensual pleasure.' So a pensive, demure Selima was inappropriate. If she had been an amiable sort of cat, not a pampered favourite, the servants Tom and Susan would have kept a sharper lookout and listened to her agonizing appeals for help. Gray should have established her at once as plump and vain:

> 'Twas on a lofty vase's side,
> Where China's gayest art had dyed
>   The azure flowers that blow;
> Demurest of the tabby kind,
> The pensive Selima reclined,
>   Gazed on the lake below.

He should also have made it immediately clear that

35

Selima saw her image mirrored in the water (which was doubtless why he preferred a China vase to a glass tub that would not have provided the necessary reflection) and should have left the twitching tail for later:

> Her conscious tail her joy declared;
> The fair round face, the snowy beard,
>   The velvet of her paws,
> Her coat, that with the tortoise vies,
> Her ears of jet, and emerald eyes,
>   She saw; and purr'd applause.

Declared and *beard* are not close enough rhymes for such neat drawing-room verse; and to secure a rhyme for *eyes*, he has awkwardly changed the tense in *vies* from past to present (although Selima is already dead before the poem ends). But to change *vies* to *vied* and rhyme it with *pride* meant repeating the *ide*-rhyme of the first stanza. And *coat with tortoise shell that vies* is an awkward inversion. Moreover, *saw and purred applause* is an unmusical line.

At this point Gray adopted the then popular mock-heroic style:

> Still had she gazed; but 'midst the tide
> Two angel forms were seen to glide,
>   The Genii of the stream:
> Their scaly armour's Tyrian hue
> Thro' richest purple to the view
>   Betray'd a golden gleam.

This is shocking! Either the water is lakelike and unmoving or else it is a stream. Gray cannot make up his mind.

> Still had she gazed; but 'midst the tide. . . .

He is back again in the *ide*-rhyme but, having avoided them in the last stanza, he didn't care so much. Nevertheless his ear was, I believe, offended by all the long *i*'s of his first draft:

> . . . 'midst the tide
> Two forms divine were seen to glide,
> The Genii of the stream . . .

and he therefore substituted *angel forms* for *forms divine*. An unhappy decision, because angels fly; they never wet their wings, and they always bring messages, as these do not.

> Their scaly armour's Tyrian hue
> Thro' richest purple to the view
> Betray'd a golden gleam. . . .

Thro' richest purple to the view is shameless padding for the sake of the rhyme; nor do goldfish have a Tyrian purple aspect when seen in a China vase. I should like to believe that Gray was thinking of the golden Mediterranean amber which (unlike Baltic amber) has a distinct purple gleam, and which the Tyrian merchants prized; but this is most unlikely.

> The hapless Nymph with wonder saw:
> A whisker first and then a claw,
>   With many an ardent wish,
> She stretch'd in vain to reach the prize.
> What female heart can gold despise?
>   What Cat's averse to fish?

Here we have even shoddier verse. The second line reads like the object of *saw*. *With many an ardent wish* is peculiarly feeble, and one knows from a mile away that the rhyme *fish* is coming. Selima did not stretch a

37

whisker or a claw; she will have stretched her neck and paw. Gray could have combined these last two stanzas into one, and lost nothing but mere length:

> Presumptuous Maid! with looks intent
> Again she stretch'd, again she bent,
>   Nor knew the gulf between.
> (Malignant Fate sat by, and smiled.)
> The slipp'ry verge her feet beguiled,
>   She tumbled headlong in.

The hapless Nymph with wonder saw . . . comes too close after *Presumptuous Maid! with looks intent.* . . . Both are unnecessary to the argument. *Nor knew the gulf between* . . . is unclear. Did this gulf lie between herself and the fish, or between the fish and the surface? And *between* rhymes badly with *in*.

> (Malignant Fate sat *by*, and *smiled*.)

More long *i*'s; and *her* refers grammatically not to Selima but to Fate, whom he should have put in the plural.

> Eight times emerging from the flood
> She mew'd to ev'ry wat'ry god,
>   Some speedy aid to send.
> No Dolphin came, no Nereid stirr'd:
> Nor cruel Tom, nor Susan heard.
>   A fav'rite has no friend!

The water, hitherto described as a lake, a stream with genii, and a tide, now appears as a flood: to rhyme, more or less, with *wat'ry god*. Dolphins, though sacred to Apollo, are not gods; nor would a dolphin fit easily into even the largest-sized Chinese vase. 'Triton' should match *Nereid*.

From hence, ye Beauties undeceived,
Know, one false step is ne'er retrieved,
    And be with caution bold.
Not all that tempts your wand'ring eyes
And heedless hearts is lawful prize;
    Nor all that glisters, gold.

Beauties undeceived should mean that they see through shams; but what Gray evidently intends is 'not yet undeceived by disaster'. And *heedless hearts* is wrong. He means 'greedy hearts'—*heedless* should go with ears. *And be with caution bold* is too elliptic a phrase.

Now, although all this may be negative criticism, you can hardly challenge me to rewrite a poem which is not mine, and which I could never have been tempted to write. I can guess how unpopular I already am for having spoiled your early love of this playful piece—which, at any rate, did not bore you, as for example Gray himself did, with his *Pindaric Ode, The Progress of Poesy:*

    Awake, Aeolian lyre, awake,
    And give to rapture all thy trembling strings.
    From Helicon's harmonious springs
        A thousand rills their mazy progress take:
    The laughing flowers, that round them blow,
    Drink life and fragrance as they flow.
    Now the rich stream of music winds along
    Deep, majestic, smooth and strong,
    Thro' verdant vales, and Ceres' golden reign:
    Now rolling down the steep amain,
    Headlong, impetuous see it pour;
    The rocks and nodding groves rebellow to the roar.

Nevertheless, I am prepared to be more unpopular still by accepting the challenge and suggesting improvements to the Cat poem:

On a tall vase's curving side
By Pekin's potters beautified
   With flowers of azure hue,
Most pampered of her tabby sort
Plump Selima reclined in sport
   The lake beneath to view.

As in a looking-glass appeared
Her fair round face and snowy beard,
   The velvet of her paws,
Her coat, which vied with tortoiseshell,
Black ears and emerald eyes; ' 'tis well,'
   Thought she, and purred applause.

Her long tail twitched; for, ah, behold
Athwart the image, scaled with gold
   Two creatures swam in sight!
What young heart goes not pit-a-pat
At sight of specie? For what cat
   Are fishes no delight?

Fond creature! On the prize intent
She dipped a paw and forward bent
   To hook some tail or fin;
Malignant Fates, observing, smiled,
The slippery verge her feet beguiled,
   She tumbled headlong in.

Eight times from death she drowning rose
And mewed a piteous prayer to those
   Who aid divine could send.
No Triton came, no Nereid stirred—
Though maybe Tom or Susan heard,
   A favourite has no friend.

Learn, maids by fraud yet undeceived,
That one false move is ne'er retrieved.
   Then cautious be, though bold.

Not all that tempts your greedy eyes
And wandering thoughts is lawful prize,
    Nor all that glisters, gold.

An important rule of craftsmanship in English Verse is
that a poet should never tell his readers how romantic,
pathetic, awe-inspiring, tragic, mystic or wondrous a
scene has been. He must describe the details himself in
such powerful but restrained language (nouns and verbs
always outnumbering the adjectives), that it will be the
reader who catches his breath, looks up from the page
and says: 'How romantic, how pathetic, how awe-
inspiring, how . . .!'
Longfellow, a sweet, simple, loving but poetically in-
effective New Englander, often breaks this rule:

Ah! what pleasant visions haunt me
    As I gaze upon the sea!
All the old romantic legends,
    All my dreams come back to me.

Sails of silk and ropes of sandal,
    Such as gleam in ancient lore;
And the singing of the sailors,
    And the answer from the shore!

Most of all, the Spanish ballad
    Haunts me oft, and tarries long,
Of the noble Count Arnaldos
    And the sailor's mystic song.

Telling how the Count Arnaldos,
    With his hawk upon his hand,
Saw a fair and stately galley,
    Steering onward to the land;—

How he heard the ancient helmsman
    Chant a song so wild and clear,

That the sailing sea-bird slowly
Poised upon the mast to hear.

Till his soul was full of longing,
  And he cried, with impulse strong,—
'Helmsman! for the love of heaven,
  Teach me, too, that wondrous song!'

'Wouldst thou,'—so the helmsman answered,—
'Learn the secret of the sea?
Only those who brave its dangers
Comprehend its mystery!'

What a second-hand way of telling the story! Pleasant visions haunt Longfellow sometimes as he gazes on the Atlantic Ocean from Casco Bay, Massachusetts; literary reminiscences, especially of a Spanish ballad—he spent a few months in Spain in the late 1820s—echo in his ears. But he records only a sentimental gist of the ballad, not the ballad itself.

Ropes of sandal such as gleam in ancient lore . . .
Haunts me oft and tarries long . . .

The pay-off: *Only those who brave its dangers Comprehend its mystery!* is in the pure style of *Hymns, Ancient and Modern.* The reader doesn't care a button for Longfellow's feelings; he wants to hear the original ballad or, if he can't read Spanish, its equivalent in English.

I have taken the trouble to look up the ballad, which was originally written in twelfth-century Catalan— *Canço del Compte l'Arnau;* but the version Longfellow recalled was a Castilian one, published in the 1550 edition of the *Cancionero de Romances.* If Longfellow had contrived to curb his New England corniness, and written a translation of the ballad closer to the traditional English style than his famous *Schooner Hesperus*, it would have run something like this:

> O the bold Lord Arnold, what did he hear
> That midsummer day in the morning clear?
>
> Lord Arnold rode with hawk upon hand
> And down he coursed to the salt sea strand.
>
> He saw a galley—I tell no lies—
> Was making the beach before his eyes!
>
> Her sails were silk, of sandal her gear,
> And a practised mariner took the steer.
>
> He trolled so wild and he trolled so well
> He fetched all nature under a spell,
>
> The winds were bated and no more blew
> That calm as a mere the salt sea grew.
>
> O, the fish schooled up, it was thick and fast,
> And sea-cobs perched on the galley's mast.
>
> 'O mariner good who has ta'en the steer
> And trollest a song that I love to hear,
>
> 'Do but teach me to sing that same, pardie,
> And a chest of treasure thou's earn in fee.'
>
> 'Nay, songs there are that a helmsman sings
> May never be boughten with bright shillings,
>
> 'And mine's a ditty of worth, pardie,
> Taught only to who dare sail with me.'

You will observe that Longfellow's memories of the

ballad have played him false. In the original there are no sailors but only a helmsman; and not a single gull perches on the mast, but flocks of them; also the winds and seas are calmed, and the fish swim up in shoals. The helmsman is not ancient, nor does he make any moralistic remarks about the mystery of the sea; and the ship appears—this is most important—on St John's Day, namely Midsummer Day, when one should expect magical apparitions. The helmsman will have been Herne the Hunter, whose oak occurs in Shakespeare's *Midsummer Night's Dream*—or Herne's Spanish equivalent; and he was tempting Arnaldos the hunter with melodies of a pagan fairyland. Herne and Hermes Trismegistos, who conveyed souls to the paradise of the mystics, are the same divine character.

While I am on the subject: Longfellow's line, *He cried with impulse strong*, reminds me that, while still an undergraduate here in 1922, I published a book called *On English Poetry*, from which I will quote a paragraph:

An old Italian portrait-painter, coming to the end of his life, gathered his friends and pupils together and revealed to them a great discovery he had made, as follows: 'The art of portrait painting consists in putting the High Lights at exactly the right place in the eyes.' When I come to my death bed, I have a similarly important message to deliver: 'The art of poetry consists in knowing exactly how to manipulate the letter S.'

Of all well-known poets of the nineteenth century, Shelley was perhaps the most deficient in his control of sibilants. His *Ode to the West Wind* contains such lines as:

All overgrown with azure moss and flowers
So sweet the sense faints picturing them . . .

and:

44

When to outstrip thy skiey speed
Scarce seemed a vision . . .

Thou on whose streams mid the steep sky's commotion,
Loose clouds like earth's decaying leaves are shed. . . .

*

Quiller-Couch admitted Longfellow and Poe into the *Oxford Book of English Verse* to prove he was no more snobbish about English poems written in America, than about those written in Scotland or Ireland, so long as they accepted the verse-standards set at Oxford, Cambridge and London. This rule excluded Robert Frost and e. e. cummings, although both came into his period. He granted Longfellow another poem, *Chaucer*, which recalls the Poet Laureate's recent *Homage to Shakespeare* and seems to have been written in perfect idleness of spirit:

An old man in a lodge within a park;
    The chamber walls depicted all around
    With portraitures of huntsman, hawk, and hound,
    And the hurt deer. He listeneth to the lark,
Whose song comes with the sunshine through the dark
    Of painted glass in leaden lattice bound;
    He listeneth and he laugheth at the sound,
    Then writeth in a book like any clerk.
He is the poet of the dawn, who wrote
    The Canterbury Tales, and his old age
    Made beautiful with song; and as I read
I hear the crowing cock, I hear the note
    Of lark and linnet, and from every page
    Rise odours of plough'd field or flowery mead.

An old man in a lodge within a park—*at* a lodge within a park would have been neater—perhaps North

Petterton Park, Somerset, of which Chaucer was appointed Forester in late middle age but which is unlikely to have been his residence; its chamber walls depicted with portraitures of animals. . . . We wait for the main verb, but are disappointed. Animals, by the way, in English, can be depicted *on* a wall; but a wall cannot be depicted *with* pictures. If he means 'hung with an arras', why not say so? The animals include a hurt deer—*hurt* is used rather of injured feelings than of physical injuries —perhaps Longfellow remembers the sequester'd stag in *As You Like It* that from the hunters' aim had ta'en a hurt and wept big round tears into the swift brook. 'Stricken' or 'wounded' is what was meant, but he has not left himself enough room for it in the line. 'He *listeneth* to the lark, Whose song *comes*' (why not 'cometh'?) with the sunshine through the dark of painted glass. . . . *Dark* is used for the sake of the rhyme and misdirects the reader into recalling St Paul's 'as through a glass, darkly'. 'In leaden lattice *bound*' has also been used for the sake of the rhyme, which should never be allowed to obscure or divert the sense.

He listeneth to the lark, and he laugheth, then he writeth like any clerk. . . . What does *like any clerk* mean? In Chaucer's time it could have meant that, though an uneducated man, he had somehow surreptitiously learned to read and write. Chaucer, however, was very much of a clerk: being Royal Comptroller of Customs and often sent abroad on diplomatic missions.

He is the poet of the dawn. . . . What dawn? Real or metaphorical? And, yes, everyone knows that he wrote *The Canterbury Tales.*

And as I read, I hear the crowing cock. . . . Is this metaphorical of the dawn? And is Longfellow himself reading at an early hour? Or is he referring to Chauntecler in *The Nun-Priest's Tale?* He also hears *the note of lark and linnet.* . . . We can grant Chaucer knowledge of larks, though he used them only in the plural—*flocks of laverockes and turtles* occur in the *Romaunt of the Rose*— but 'linnet' enters English literature only a century and a half later. In Longfellow's time, because of its rhyming facility—'linnet', 'minute', 'begin it', 'in it', 'win it', and so on—the linnet ousted from anthologies the chaffinch, bullfinch, redstart and all other small passerine birds. 'Red-poll', the linnet's proper name when wearing summer-plumage, hardly ever appears. . . . No amount of repair work could make a prize poem of this sonnet.

*

Edgar Allan Poe's verses entranced the late Victorian English. The English always take pity on drunken, ill-living and unbalanced poets as soon as they are dead. Here is Poe's famous *To Helen:*

> Helen, thy beauty is to me
>   Like those Nicean barks of yore
> That gently, o'er a perfumed sea,
>   The weary way-worn wanderer bore
>   To his own native shore.
>
> On desperate seas long wont to roam,
>   Thy hyacinth hair, thy classic face,
> Thy Naiad airs have brought me home
>   To the glory that was Greece,
>   And the grandeur that was Rome.
>
> Lo, in yon brilliant window-niche
>   How statue-like I see thee stand,
>   The agate lamp within thy hand,
> Ah! Psyche, from the regions which
>   Are holy land!

He addresses Helen, whose name is evocative of ships,

47

though the real Helen sent over a thousand ships away and brought few back. The Nicean barks are unclassical. The most important Nicaea, a Hellenistic city in Bithynia, lay inland on a lake; the second was built by Alexander the Great on the banks of the Jelum in India; the third, now Nice, was of no importance at all in Graeco-Roman times. Which is intended? Probably Poe knew of the Nicaean Creed, and used the word because it sounded nice.

The argument of the poem is that the Classical beauty of a girl named Helen has brought Poe home over a perfumed sea—which? Black Sea, Mediterranean or Indian Ocean?—though long wont to roam in desperate ones—which, again?—to the glory that was Greece and the grandeur that was Rome.

The craftsmanship of the poem is shoddy. In the first stanza, *weary, wayworn, wanderer bore* gives excessive alliteration; and *worn* and *bore* are too similar in sound. The second stanza is clumsily inverted:

> On desperate seas long wont to roam,
> Thy hyacinth hair, thy classic face,
> Thy Naiad airs have brought me home
> To the glory that was Greece,
> And the grandeur that was Rome . . .

so that it seems that Helen's hyacinth hair and classic face are long wont to roam on desperate seas. The explanation seems to be that Poe has attempted to hide the false rhyme of *Rome . . . roam* by keeping them as far away from each other as possible. In English, *hyacinth hair* means blue hair; but here it apparently stands for 'hyacinthine', an adjective borrowed by English poets from 'locks like the hyacinth flower'—a metaphor coined by Homer to whom, some grammarians say, it meant black; and some, gold.

In the third stanza Poe switches from Helen to the Psyche of Apuleius' *Golden Ass* as portrayed by a Royal Academician. It does not keep up the rich variation of vowel sounds that he has used hitherto:

> Lo, in yon brilliant window-niche
> How statue-like I see thee stand,
> The agate lamp within thy hand,
> Ah! Psyche, from the regions which
> Are holy land!

He gives us three short *i*'s in a row—*brilliant, window, niche*—then five short *a*'s—*statue, stand, agate, lamp, hand*. The subject of the phrase *from the regions which Are holy land!* is hard to discover. Since it cannot be Psyche herself—one can't *stand* from regions—it may be the agate lamp. . . . But what Poe means is anyone's guess. The lamp in Apuleius' allegory served only to burn Cupid with its drop of scalding oil, and get Psyche into desperate trouble.

*

Quiller-Couch claims to have included in his anthology no single epigram which 'failed to preserve some thrill of the emotion through which it had to pass before the Muse's lips let it fall, with however exquisite deliberation'. Let us take a look at a couple of pieces by Walter Savage Landor, who was renowned as an epigrammatist:

> Ah, what avails the sceptred race!
> Ah, what the form divine!
> What every virtue, every grace!
> Rose Aylmer, all were thine.

> Rose Aylmer, whom these wakeful eyes
> May weep, but never see,
> A night of memories and sighs
> I consecrate to thee.

This is a private poem; the poet has deliberately suppressed every clue to its meaning and instead given us a false clue, calling the woman whom he celebrates, by a false name. The sentences beginning with *Ah, what* end in 'notes of admiration'—as they were called in Landor's day—rather than notes of interrogation. Yet they cannot be spoken except as questions, and seem to mean: 'What is the good of having royal blood, or being divinely beautiful, or possessing every grace and virtue? None of all this helped poor Rose Aylmer.'

The second stanza:

> Rose Aylmer, whom these wakeful eyes
> May weep, but never see,
> A night of memories and sighs
> I consecrate to thee . . .

explains that he may never see Rose, though he may perhaps weep for her; and will dedicate a whole night of memories and sighs to thinking about her.

Well, what happened? Did she die? But, if so, why 'may never see'? *May* can imply either possibility or permission. If possibility, perhaps she went into a nunnery where royal blood and graceful social virtues were at a discount, and the poet felt it unlikely that he would be allowed to see her, even through a grille. Or perhaps he had gone blind? Or, since he does not say 'may never see you again', does *may* simply mean that God had not permitted a meeting, by separating them in time? Is she a historical character, or even a fictional character, with whom he has fallen in love? If Rose Aylmer were a surrogate, say, for Lady Jane Grey, who had every virtue and grace and came of royal blood, but was executed for high treason because someone had injudiciously proclaimed her Queen of England—that would make sense. A sensitive Victorian, falling in love with her portrait,

might easily dedicate a night of tears and sighs to historical memories of her fate. But why choose 'Rose Aylmer',
a name lacking in the true genealogical bouquet? Is it
perhaps an accident that Jane's tutor was John Aylmer,
afterwards Bishop of London? Try it this way:

ON ADMIRING A MINIATURE OF LADY JANE GREY

> Ah, what availed the sceptred race?
> Ah, what the form divine?
> What every virtue, every grace?
> Sweet Lady, all were thine!
>
> By Aylmer tutored in the arts
> To be a very sage;
> Yet smiling sovereign of all hearts,
> And Rose of her rude age.
>
> Ah, Jane, whom my adoring eyes
> Weep, but may never see,
> A night of retrospective sighs
> I'll consecrate to thee.

*

No epigram stands up unless, like most of those in the
Greek Anthology, or those Latin ones quoted by Sueto-
nius, it is absolutely succinct. How much of Landor's
Proud Word You Never Spoke could be omitted without
damage to the sense?

> Proud word you never spoke, but you will speak
> Four not exempt from pride some future day.
> Resting on one white hand a warm wet cheek,
> Over my open volume you will say,
> 'This man loved *me*'—then rise and trip away.

51

Four not exempt from pride is too succinct. He means 'exempt from a charge of pride'. But why not:

> Proud word you never spoke, but you will speak
> Four, some future day?

And why *future? Will speak* is in the future tense. Why not: 'Four, some day'?

> Resting on one white hand a warm wet cheek. . . .

All that matters is that she has been crying; the whiteness and warmness are irrelevant. Both cheeks will have been equally warm and wet, and all ladies in those days kept their hands out of the sun. 'Tearfully, your head propped on one elbow' is the required sense. But why prophesy her posture?

You will speak, followed by *you will say*, is clumsy. And which *open volume?* It may have been a volume of sermons, or a travel book, or a scientific monograph. . . . The reader must realize that it is a book of poems written to the girl with the warm, wet cheek, under the Landorian *nom de plume* of 'Ianthe', 'Dirce' or 'Clementina'.

Then rise and trip away is unnecessary; and *trip* seems too jaunty a gait in the circumstances. She will surely have stumbled away to her bedroom—this was before the time of bathrooms—and washed her face in cold water? But perhaps Landor wishes to think of her as still young and beautiful after his death: hence *trip*. Also the reader should not be asked to count four words. Three is better; one does not count numbers up to three. To convert this into a Classical epigram, the lines must be shortened and reduced to a four-line stanza:

> You are not proud, yet I can hear you speak
> Three words of pride, one day,

Over this book: tears dewing either cheek,
'He loved me,' you will say.

Landor's epigram *Verse* cannot be remedied, since no
real emotion underlies it:

Past ruin'd Ilion Helen lives,
    Alcestis rises from the shades;
Verse calls them forth; 'tis verse that gives
    Immortal youth to mortal maids.

Soon shall Oblivion's deepening veil
    Hide all the peopled hills you see,
The gay, the proud, while lovers hail
    These many summers you and me.

Landor misdirects his readers throughout this poem.
Past ruin'd Ilion Helen lives. . . . To begin with, even if
they recognize 'Ilium' as a poetic synonym for 'Troy',
used by Marlowe and others, *Ilion*, the Greek form, will
puzzle them. Next, *past* is ambiguous. If I were to tell
you casually: 'Helen is living past the ruined church,'
your natural conclusion would be that my friend Helen
had a house on the road past the ruined church. But *past*
here apparently means that Helen—Queen Helen, not
just any Helen—has survived the sack of Troy. Having
got at least so far, one says: 'Yes, that's right. Helen did
survive for many years, and eventually settled down
happily with Menelaus at Sparta.'
    Alcestis rises from the shades. . . . 'Yes,' one says again.
'That's right. Although Alcestis had consented to die for
her husband Admetus's sake, Heracles rescued her from
Death's clutches and brought her safe home again. So
she and Helen had something in common: both arrived
safely home after a lot of trouble.'
    Then comes the line *Verse calls them forth* . . . and

with it the realization that we have been misdirected.
Neither Helen nor Alcestis was rescued from trouble by
Orpheus's charmed singing. Landor comments:

> 'tis verse that gives
> Immortal youth to mortal maids. . . .

So Helen and Alcestis have, after all, been chosen at
random as Greek heroines—they might just as well have
been Nausicaa or Iphigeneia or Ariadne—and Landor is
merely reminding us that Greek poets have perpetuated
the youth of long dead women! Or does *gives immortal
youth to mortal maids* mean that Apollo as a beardless
youth, ever fair and young, charms mortal girls when his
poets are inspired by him?

The second stanza is a real mess;

> Soon shall Oblivion's deepening veil
> Hide all the peopled hills you see,
> The gay, the proud, while lovers hail
> These many summers you and me . . .

Landor says that *you*—whoever this *you* may be—will
soon forget all about the peopled hills you see. Can he
mean the seven hills of Rome?—for hills are not usually
peopled. His next four words, *The gay, the proud*, can
hardly refer to the hills, and grammatically go with the
you contemplating them; if so, the proud and gay are
being contrasted with the lovers who hail *you and me*,
and who must therefore be conceived as humbly, gloom-
ily, but memorably alive in a valley or on a plain. This
you can hardly be the same *you*, and we are led to guess,
but cannot be sure, that the lovers are hailing Landor as
the poet, and Ianthe as the young woman to whom he
has given immortal youth in his verse.

Charles Lamb's *Old Familiar Faces* is included by

Quiller-Couch. The recurrent line, *All, all are gone, the old familar faces*, is thought to justify by its pathos the rambling incompetence of the argument:

I have had playmates, I have had companions,
In my days of childhood, in my joyful school-days—
All, all are gone, the old familiar faces.

I have been laughing, I have been carousing,
Drinking late, sitting late, with bosom cronies—
All, all are gone, the old familiar faces.

I loved a Love once, fairest among women:
Closed are her doors on me, I must not see her—
All, all are gone, the old familiar faces.

I have a friend, a kinder friend has no man:
Like an ingrate, I left my friend abruptly;
Left him, to muse on the old familiar faces.

Ghost-like I paced round the haunts of my childhood,
Earth seemed a desert I was bound to traverse,
Seeking to find the old familiar faces.

Friend of my bosom, thou more than a brother,
Why wert not thou born in my father's dwelling?
So might we talk of the old familiar faces—

How some they have died, and some they have left me,
And some are taken from me; all are departed—
All, all are gone, the old familiar faces.

The companions are childhood playmates who all in turn have disappeared. Eventually Lamb makes a friend, the kindest in the world, more than a brother, but leaves him abruptly and revisits the haunts of his childhood where he moons about like a ghost. The friend, not having been born in Lamb's own dwelling, falls short of perfection; he is unable to appreciate Lamb's sorrow for those who have died, or deserted, or been removed from him. Unfortunately for the reader, Lamb has not kept the story straight. The old familiar faces are here enlarged to include grown-up cronies with whom he used to drink and sit up late, and a beautiful woman who, for some unexplained reason, has closed her doors on him.

Lamb certainly could not complain of having been deserted by all his childhood friends: his sister Mary, and Coleridge who had been at school with him at Christ's Hospital, remained very close to him until his death. There was a childhood's playmate, Ann Simmons, met when he went on holidays to Widmore, for whom he later wrote sonnets. It is even suggested that because she would not marry him, his mind became temporarily unhinged and he was briefly committed to an asylum. But that the poem is modelled on Horace's *Odes* suggests the bosom-cronies to have been fellow-scholars from his beloved Christ's Hospital—Wordsworth? Leigh Hunt?— whereas the beloved friend had unfortunately not studied there with him.

> I have had playmates, I have had companions
> In my days of childhood, in my joyful schooldays.
> All, all are gone, the old familiar faces . . .

should surely read:

> Once I had playmates, once I had companions

And:

> So we might talk of the old familiar faces
> How some have died and some they have left me,
> And some are taken from me . . .

could easily be improved by half a minute's care. Thus:

> How this one is dead, and that one has left me,
> A third taken from me.

And *Why wert thou not born in my father's dwelling?* is extravagant. For the friend to have been born merely 'in the self-same village' would surely suffice. A simple omission of the stanzas about the bosom cronies and the beautiful woman would make sense of the poem: though only as a macabre account of what would now be called 'a regressive infantile fixation'.

*

The Reverend Robert Herrick is an endearing character: the jolly anti-Puritan parson who encouraged his parishioners to keep England merry, who would give a favourite sow ale from a silver tankard and who, when rudely extruded from his cure, never wrote again; even on his return at the glorious Restoration. But Herrick's verse shows little care. His most famous song *Gather Ye Rosebuds While Ye May* fails to satisfy even casual scrutiny, and no melody however bewitching could blind us to the demerits of at least one of its four stanzas:

> Gather ye rosebuds while ye may,
>   Old Time is still a-flying:
> And this same flower that smiles to-day
>   To-morrow will be dying.
>
> The Glorious lamp of heaven, the sun,
>   The higher he's a-getting,
> The sooner will his race be run,
>   And nearer he's to setting.
>
> That age is best that is the first,
>   When youth and blood are warmer;

But being spent, the worse, and worst
Times still succeed the former.

Then be not coy, but use your time,
And while ye may, go marry:
For having lost but once your prime,
You may for ever tarry.

Old Time is still a-flying? Why *old*? *Old Time* conjures up an image of Father Time with scythe and hour-
glass, who creeps rather than flies. Herrick means, in
fact, that the time of youth, not Old Time, is flying. The
words *Old Time*, moreover, are hard to sing. And
Herrick's near-contemporary Milton would have frowned
at *Time, flying, smiles; rose, old; same, to-day*, which
sadly reduce the variation of vowels called for by so
pretty a start.

Here, for comparison, are a few lines from Milton's
Arcades, to show how verse should be written:

O're the smooth enameld green
Where no print of step hath been,
Follow me as I sing,
And touch the warbléd string.
Under the shady roof
Of branching Elm Star-proof,
   Follow me,
I will bring you where she sits
Clad in splendor as befits
   Her deity.
Such a rural Queen
All Arcadia hath not seen.

One can't fault Milton in sound—he was a musician
manqué—though, as I have observed elsewhere, when
his sound and sense are in conflict, the sense always
loses. *Touch the warbléd string*, for example, is in-
defensible.

In *Gather Ye Rosebuds* the sense as well as the sound is ill-used. *This same flower*, presumably a rosebud, does not die within twenty-four hours of its first opening—unless in exceptionally severe weather; though roses already in full bloom have a shorter life, and the word *to-morrow* would fit their case.

The second stanza is simple to the point of fatuousness; contains too many *the*'s; and is syntactically unbalanced at the close:

> The glorious lamp of heaven, the sun,
>   The higher he's a-getting,
> The sooner will his race be run,
>   And nearer he's to setting. . . .

The third stanza is on the same pattern, but more carelessly written:

> That age is best which is the first,
>   When youth and blood are warmer;
> But being spent, the worse, and worst
>   Times still succeed the former. . . .

That age is best which is the first, should refer to the first of the Seven Ages of Man, or Woman. The construction of the third and fourth lines raises difficulties for the singer, who must pause an awkwardly long time between *But being spent* and *the worse*, to keep them from combining in a wrong sense. And *worst times still* is the sort of syzygy (meaning the connection between the end of one word and the start of the next, as one speaks them) which cannot be admitted in any song.

The final stanza runs:

> Then be not coy, but use your time,
>   And while ye may, go marry;

> For having lost but once your prime,
>> You may for ever tarry. . . .

This adds nothing to the first stanza, and has other weaknesses. *Your time* and *Old Time* are unrelated in sense. Nor are the two *may*'s parallel. *While you may* means 'while ye still can', whereas *you may for ever tarry* means 'it is possible that you will tarry'. As a Spaniard answered me once when I asked: 'Can visitors go into that convent?', 'They can, but they don't may.' Again, *For having lost but once your prime*, is difficult to sing; and *but once* is introduced solely to pad out the metre. 'Having lost your prime' would be quite enough. And why does *ye* turn into *you?* The convention that *ye* is nominative, and *you* accusative, has been broken.

Most of these points are negligible by themselves, but in mass they detract from the poem's value. If Herrick had taken more trouble, he would have written something like this; but better, of course, because it was his poem, not mine:

> Gather ye rosebuds while ye may—
>> Their time is fast a-flying
> And many a bloom that's blown today
>> Tomorrow will be dying.

> That glorious Lamp of Heaven, the Sun,
>> The nearer noon he's getting,
> The earlier will his race be run
>> And swifter fall the setting.

> Then seize the forelock of Old Time
>> And while ye may, go marry:
> Lest, having missed your lovesome prime,
>> Ye should for ever tarry.

*

Fortunately several songs included in the anthology are written by poets with a sensitive ear for music. James VI of Scotland's courtier Alexander Montgomerie, for example, in his *The Night Is Near Gone:*

Hey! now the day dawis;
The jolly cock crawis;
Now shroudis the shawis
  Thro' Nature anon.
The thissel-cock cryis
On lovers wha lyis:
Now skaillis the skyis;
  The nicht is neir gone.

The fieldis ouerflowis
With gowans that growis,
Quhair lilies like low is
  As red as the rone.
The turtle that true is,
With notes that renewis,
Her pairty pursuis:
  The nicht is neir gone.

Now hairtis with hindis
Conform to their kindis,
Hie tursis their tyndis
  On ground quhair they grone.
Now hurchonis, with hairis,
Ays passis in pairis;
Quhilk duly declaris
  The nicht is neir gone. . . .

It is the neatest, prettiest, rightest, most varied in sound of any Tudor song I know.

Thomas Campion, Montgomerie's English contemporary, made sure of his words by writing their music himself. Though not nearly so lively as Montgomerie's, because the music seems to have dictated them, they do read sensibly, at least:

Now Winter nights enlarge
   The number of their hours,
And clouds their storms discharge
   Upon the airy towers.
Let now the chimneys blaze
   And cups o'erflow with wine;
Let well-tunéd words amaze
   With harmony divine.
Now yellow waxen lights
   Shall wait on honey love,
While youthful revels, masques, and courtly sights
   Sleep's leaden spells remove.

This time doth well dispense
   With lovers' long discourse;
Much speech hath some defence,
   Though beauty no remorse.
All do not all things well;
   Some measures comely tread,
Some knotted riddles tell,
   Some poems smoothly read.
The summer hath his joys,
   And winter his delights;
Though love and all his pleasures are but toys,
   They shorten tedious nights.

LECTURE THREE

Lecture Three, 1964

I never considered the arts of Latin and Greek Verse taught me at my public school as bearing any relation to poetry. Nor, I think, did any master or fellow-pupil. To the Oxford University awards for verse-competitions in these dead languages the Newdigate Prize has been added which, as I noted in my first lecture, Matthew Arnold won with a poem about Cromwell. It seems to have been Sir Roger Newdigate's hope to encourage proficiency in the writing of English heroic couplets, Miltonic blank verse, or Pindaric Odes; and as an *ex officio* judge of the Prize, I should feel bound to respect his wishes, if the candidates did likewise. In the last three years, however, the only compositions submitted in the old-fashioned style have fallen so far short even of early nineteenth-century standards, that my fellow-judges and I have either withheld the prize or crowned a candidate who showed a certain sincerity and an understanding of the proper use of English; and whose poem would neither bore nor shock the Heads of Houses, doctors and graduates assembled in the Sheldonian at the Encaenia.

For Sir Roger, a liberal-minded colliery owner, and for others like him, what is actually said has always seemed less important than the decorous formality of its expression. As soon as Jacobinism and the Romantic Revival invited English poets to break the verse conventions borrowed from France at the Restoration, everyone went a different way. Some adopted the precepts of Ben Jonson, our first and best Poetic Laureate, who chose words carefully for their emotional force, history, exact connotation, sound, texture, and weight; and at the *Mermaid*

65

in London, and over at Lord Falkland's house at Great Tew, taught young poets this essential craft. Wordsworth and Coleridge, at their best, followed Jonson. Others, such as Keats, compromised by building up a more ornate verse convention, largely based on Spenser and the later Milton. Still others, like Shelley, felt sanctioned to write whatever they pleased in any metre that occurred to them. All of them, however, were sufficiently traditional to write set pieces: Odes to Melancholy, Autumn, Duty, the West Wind, the Departing Year, Solitude, the Mediterranean Sea, and so forth.

I despise Odes, myself, as wholly unilateral. Neither Melancholy, Autumn, Duty, the West Wind, the Departing Year, Solitude, nor the Mediterranean Sea itself, can answer or even acknowledge these addresses. And odes or sonnets to the dead are ruled by the consideration of *De mortuis nil nisi bonum*—or, as Hilaire Belloc once rewrote the tag: *De mortuis, cui bono?*

The *Oxford Book of English Verse* contains Wordsworth's *Sonnet to Milton:*

> Milton! thou shouldst be living at this hour:
> England hath need of thee: she is a fen
> Of stagnant waters: altar, sword, and pen,
> Fireside, the heroic wealth of hall and bower,
> Have forfeited their ancient English dower
> Of inward happiness. We are selfish men;
> O raise us up, return to us again,
> And give us manners, virtue, freedom, power!
> Thy soul was like a Star, and dwelt apart;
> Thou hadst a voice whose sound was like the sea:
> Pure as the naked heavens, majestic, free,
> So didst thou travel on life's common way,
> In cheerful godliness; and yet thy heart
> The lowliest duties on herself did lay.

Did Wordsworth really mean this? Or did he plume

himself on having succeeded Milton as poetic Mentor to the English nation, and write this in vindication of his claim? Surely he is congratulating himself because he also has a soul like a Star, and dwells apart in the Lake District? Yet Milton did not have a soul like a Star; nor did he give England manners, virtue, freedom, power; nor did he even dwell apart—until forced to do so by blindness and the Restoration. Either Wordsworth is most ill-read in history, or he is advocating what would now be called 'undisguised Fascism'. During the Civil War, Milton had written his famous *Areopagitica* (a plea for the freedom of the Press) but afterwards became Assistant Press Censor for the Council of State and helped to enforce a most repressive Censorship Law. This Council of State, you will remember, was the executive branch of a minority government set up by the mutinous New Model Army, after they had suppressed the House of Lords, and forcibly reduced the Commons by a purge of the conservative majority to a small group of Independents—the Rump—who would co-operate in the execution of the King and the abolition of the monarchy.

Milton's married life was ugly. He did not 'travel on life's common way in simple godliness', nor did his hall or bower keep their ancient English dower of inward happiness. . . . 'Many of his choicest years of life,' it is recorded by his nephew, 'were employed in wrangling and raquetting back conjugal reproach, accusation and sarcasm.' When his first wife left him, he tried unsuccessfully to commit bigamy. After her death he bullied his three daughters, stinted them of pocket money, and condemned them to the 'reading aloud and exact pronouncing of all the languages of whatever book he should think fit to peruse: the Hebrew (and, I think, the Syriac), the Greek, the Latin, the Italian, the Spanish, the French—of which they understood not one word . . .'. And he cut them out of his will on the ground that their mother's marriage portion had never been paid him. He had also defrauded their maternal grandmother of her 'widow's thirds'.

It is clear, however, that Wordsworth admired Milton's verse-craft, and envied him his political power under the Commonwealth, though keeping far away from Whitehall himself: he had badly blotted his copybook during the first years of the French Revolution. Take from the *Oxford Book of English Verse*, Wordsworth's *Valedictory Sonnet to the River Duddon*, and see what its sonorous majesty disguises:

I thought of Thee, my partner and my guide,
    As being pass'd away.—Vain sympathies!
    For, backward, Duddon! as I cast my eyes,
I see what was, and is, and will abide;
Still glides the Stream, and shall for ever glide;
    The Form remains, the Function never dies;
    While we, the brave, the mighty, and the wise,
We Men, who in our morn of youth defied
The elements, must vanish;—be it so!
    Enough, if something from our hands have power
    To live, and act, and serve the future hour;
And if, as toward the silent tomb we go,
    Through love, through hope, and faith's transcendent dower,
We feel that we are greater than we know.

Translated into prose this means: 'Once I wrote poems about the River Duddon, because it happened to flow near my house in Cumberland; and, on moving from the neighbourhood, considered it dead without me. I realize now that this was, in part, a mistake. It still, of course, flowed in the same bed and will continue to do so, outlasting even brave, renowned, wise men like myself—who, when young, would think nothing of going for a walk in a thunderstorm. No, I cannot compete in longevity with this stream; it will be enough if my poems poetically inspire future generations; and if, as I die full of faith, hope and charity, I feel that I have perhaps underrated my enormous poetic powers.'

*

Matthew Arnold had a pretty secure command of verse craft and as little humour as either Milton or Wordsworth, but an honest and humble heart. A friend has complained to me that it was hardly fair to underline the essential dullness of the *Thyrsis* stanzas which I read in my first lecture—entries for Apollo's annual Newdigate Prize—when Arnold had at least written *Dover Beach*. This poem does not occur in the *Oxford Book of English Verse*, but he has asked me to present it for your judgement:

> The Sea is calm tonight.
> The tide is full, the moon lies fair
> Upon the straits;—on the French coast the light
> Gleams and is gone; the cliffs of England stand,
> Glimmering and vast, out in the tranquil bay.
> Come to the window, sweet is the night-air!
> Only, from the long line of spray
> Where the sea meets the moon-blanch'd land,
> Listen! you hear the grating roar
> Of pebbles which the waves draw back, and fling,
> At their return, up the high strand,
> Begin, and cease, and then again begin,
> With tremulous cadence slow, and bring
> The eternal note of sadness in.
>
> Sophocles long ago
> Heard it on the Aegean, and it brought
> Into his mind the turbid ebb and flow
> Of human misery; we
> Find also in the sound a thought,
> Hearing it by this distant northern sea.

The Sea of Faith
Was once, too, at the full, and round earth's shore
Lay like the folds of a bright girdle furl'd.
But now I only hear
Its melancholy, long, withdrawing roar,
Retreating, to the breath
Of the night-wind, down the vast edges drear
And naked shingles of the world.

Ah, love, let us be true
To one another! for the world, which seems
To lie before us like a land of dreams,
So various, so beautiful, so new,
Hath really neither joy, nor love, nor light,
Nor certitude, nor peace, nor help for pain;
And we are here as on a darkling plain
Swept with confused alarms of struggle and flight,
Where ignorant armies clash by night.

I agreed with my friend that this was a poem of genuine feeling, however miserably muddled in expression.

The moon lies fair upon the strait. The sea is calm, the tide is full: which should mean that the full moon was reflected in the water, seen from a cliff top, not from the beach, where all Arnold could have observed was its broken track on the crests of the waves. The light gleams on the French coast, and is gone. Not *a* light, but *the* light. He does not specify which. Surely, not the light of the moon? What light then? At Dover, one cannot see lights on the French coast except with a telescope from the cliff top; so Arnold's window seems certainly to be up there. Is he staying at a coast-guard's cottage? Does the gleam come from Cap Grisnez lighthouse? So far, so good. The subject of the poem is *Dover Cliffs*, not *Dover Beach*. But the cliffs are said to stand in the tranquil bay. Surely, only ships and jetties stand *in* Brighton Bay? The

cliffs enclose it. If the sea is calm, whence comes the line
of spray? Does Arnold mean 'foam' and use *spray* for the
rhyme?

He has heard in the distance the grating roar of pebbles
begin a tremulous cadence slow. How? A grating roar
can't logically begin a tremulous *cadence*, musicians
assure me, even in very modern music.

Now, for Classical reassurance, in comes Sophocles,
posted on another Aegean cliff. He too is said to have
heard the tide. Sophocles must have had good ears; there
are no observable tides in the Aegean. According to
Arnold, he likened the turbid ebb and flow of the tide to
human misery. Did he? No, he did not. He likened the
beating of a storm against the coast, with its dark tangling
weed-wrack, to the troubles experienced by mankind—
which was a different matter altogether. Arnold extends
this illegitimate metaphor to the Sea of Christian Faith,
once at full tide, but now universally at low ebb. He gets
into further trouble here by confusing the ebb and flow
of particular waves, which one can hear, with the gradual
ebb and flow of a whole tide—the sound effects of which
can be distinguished only by standing at the window for
several hours.

> The folds of a bright girdle furl'd . . .

is not only ugly in sound, and too obviously waiting for
the *world* rhyme, but inaccurate. One doesn't furl one's
girdle, like a sail or a flag, but coils it. And does *I only
hear* mean 'Only *I* hear ' or 'I only *hear*, but do not time
or count'? One can never be too careful with the word
only. Thoughts of naked shingle make Arnold clutch at
his wife in passionate despair:

> Ah, love, let us be true
> To one another. . . .

71

He means 'to each other', not *to one another*—unless both of them are schizophrenes.

The next few lines appear to mean that, although Christianity is at a low ebb, he and she must never forget their marriage vows. He complains that the world, which seems to lie before them like a land of beautiful dreams, is really a very bad place indeed. *Seems* is here used only for the rhyme; or else *dreams* is. Either the land *seems* to be a beautiful land, but isn't; or else it lies before them *like* a land of dreams. The two ideas, if run together, cancel each other out. Arnold's hysterical castigation of the world as really containing no joy, love, light, certitude, peace, or help from pain, has an almost comic ring. Are his wife and himself alone in their seemingly precarious possession of all these beautiful human abstractions?

I have never liked the pseudo-poetic *darkling*, an adverb borrowed from Milton's thrush that *sings darkling* (meaning 'in the dark') as if it were the participle from a verb 'darkle', the opposite of 'sparkle'. And even if Arnold were justified in changing the scene, at the last moment, from a moon-blanched shore to a darkling plain, armies cannot clash ignorantly by day on a darkling plain unless during an eclipse; so *darkling* is unnecessary. I wonder what battle Arnold had in mind? Perhaps it was Inkerman, the Soldiers' Battle, fought only a few years before the poem appeared, beginning at dawn on 15 November 1855, and continued murderously, though purposefully, all day by the Russians and ourselves in a haze of gunpowder smoke, both commanding generals having lost all control of their troops.

Arnold should have known better than write a poem about Dover. Keats had advised his fellow-poets against this many years before, giving as a warning example the euphoric sonnet (1802) which Wordsworth had written there after visiting Calais during a brief lull in the

Napoleonic Wars. Wordsworth sailed across to settle matters with Annette Vallon on whom, ten years before, he had fathered an illegitimate daughter, Caroline; and whom he had then heartlessly deserted in terror of having his allowance stopped by two guardian uncles. Theirs must have been an awkward encounter, because he had since been faithless not merely to her but to his revolutionary principles. However, a nice, solid, English Protestant girl, Mary Hutchinson, to whom he was now betrothed, was waiting on Dover beach to forgive his former peccadilloes and fix their marriage for October.

> Here, on our native soil, we breathe once more.
> The cock that crows, the smoke that curls, that sound
> Of bells;—those boys who in yon meadow-ground
> In white-sleeved shirts are playing; and the roar
> Of the waves breaking on the chalky shore;—
> All, all are English. Oft have I looked round
> With joy on Kent's green vales; but never found
> Myself so satisfied in heart before.
> Europe is yet in bonds; but let that pass,
> Thought for another moment. Thou art free,
> My Country! and 'tis joy enough and pride
> For one hour's perfect bliss, to tread the grass
> Of England once again, and hear and see,
> With such a dear Companion at my side.

Keats, unaware of Wordsworth's immense relief at getting safe home without forfeiting Mary's affection—which is the emotional core of the sonnet—parodied it with a random list of dislikes, to caricature Wordsworth's oversmug likes:

> The House of Mourning written by Mr Scott—
> A sermon at the Magdalen,—a tear
> Dropt on a greasy novel,—want of cheer
> After a walk uphill to a friend's cot,—
> Tea with a maiden lady,—a curs'd lot

Of worthy poems with the author near,—
A patron lord,—a drunkenness from beer,—
Haydon's great picture,—a cold coffee pot
At midnight when the Muse is ripe for labour,—
The voice of Mr Coleridge,—a french bonnet,
Before you in the pit,—a pipe and tabour,—
A damn'd inseparable flute and neighbour,—
All these are vile,—but viler Wordsworth's sonnet
On Dover: Dover! who could write upon it?

Yes, Arnold should have been warned. Wordsworth had later written an even more psychopathic sonnet at Dover, aghast at the close proximity of that vile country, France, from which God protected England (because she was so virtuous and wise) by a narrow but sufficient span of water. . . . And two others, some fifteen years after Keats's death.

*

As for Keats—Quiller-Couch omits the human Keats who wrote, for instance, the *There Was A Naughty Boy* doggerel in a letter to his sister Fanny—as distinct from the ambitious young author of *Endymion* and *Hyperion:*

(1)
There was a naughty Boy,
  A naughty boy was he,
He would not stop at home,
  He could not quiet be—
    He took
    In his Knapsack
    A Book
    Full of vowels
    And a shirt
    With some towels—
    A slight cap
    For night cap—
    A hair brush,

(2)
There was a naughty boy
  And a naughty boy was he
For nothing would he do
  But scribble poetry—
    He took
    An ink stand
    In his hand
    And a pen
    Big as ten
    In the other,
    And away
    In a Pother
    He ran

Comb ditto,
New stockings
For old ones
Would split O!
This Knapsack
Tight at's back
He rivetted close
And followed his Nose
  To the North,
  To the North,
And follow'd his nose
  To the North.

To the mountains
And fountains
And ghostes
And postes
And witches
And ditches,
And wrote
In his coat
When the weather
Was cool,
Fear of gout,
And without
When the weather
Was warm—
Och the charm
When we choose
To follow one's nose
  To the north,
  To the north,
To follow one's nose
  To the north!

(3)
There was a naughty boy
  And a naughty boy was he,
He kept little fishes
  In washing tubs three
    In spite
    Of the might
    Of the Maid
    Nor afraid
    Of his Granny-good—
    He often would
    Hurly burly
    Get up early
    And go
    By hook or crook
    To the brook
    And bring home

(4)
There was a naughty Boy,
    And a naughty Boy was he
He ran away to Scotland
    The people for to see—
    Then he found
    That the ground
    Was as hard,

75

Miller's thumb,	That a yard
Tittlebat	Was as long,
Not over fat,	That a song
Minnows small	Was as merry,
As the stall	That a cherry
Of a glove,	Was as red—
Not above	That lead
The size	Was as weighty,
Of a nice	That fourscore
Little Baby's	Was as eighty,
Little fingers—	That a door
O he made,	Was as wooden
'Twas his trade,	As in England—
Of Fish a pretty Kettle	So he stood in his shoes
A Kettle—	And he wonder'd,
A Kettle	He wonder'd,
Of Fish a pretty Kettle	He stood in his shoes
A Kettle!	And he wonder'd.

Instead we are given several of Keats's fashionable Odes, and the following 'number'—which I find a useful example of sheer bad craftsmanship:

> In a drear-nighted December,
>   Too happy, happy tree,
> Thy branches ne'er remember
>   Their green felicity:
> The north cannot undo them,
> With a sleety whistle through them;
> Nor frozen thawings glue them
>   From budding at the prime.
>
> In a drear-nighted December,
>   Too happy, happy brook,
> Thy bubblings ne'er remember
>   Apollo's summer look;
> But with a sweet forgetting,
> They stay their crystal fretting,

76

        Never, never petting
        About the frozen time.

        Ah! would 'twere so with many
        A gentle girl and boy!
        But were there ever any
        Writhed not at passèd joy?
        To know the change and feel it,
        When there is none to heal it,
        Nor numbèd sense to steal it,
        Was never said in rhyme.

The trouble begins at once:

        In a drear-nighted December,
        Too happy, happy tree,
        Thy branches ne'er remember
        Their green felicity . . .

which ninety-nine readers out of a hundred will take as
referring to the Christmas Tree in Hans Andersen's
story, made the happiest tree in the world by its decora-
tions and the cries of joy with which the children acclaim
it. And they will read the next four lines:

        The north cannot undo them,
        With a sleety whistle through them;
        Nor frozen thawings glue them
        From budding at the prime . . .

as meaning that the tree is protected against the north
wind by being placed in the parlour.

    Now, this misdirection is not altogether Keats's fault;
because Christmas trees, though common in Germany
and Denmark, were not popularized in England until
long after his death. Yet he should have stated clearly
that he had in mind the bare boughs of a deciduous tree—

a birch, or oak out on Hampstead Heath—which was happy for some other reason than the proximity of Christmas. And if a tree can be credited with memory (and why not?), it must certainly recall its green felicity; otherwise it could not repeat the annual process of successful leafing in the spring.

> In a drear-nighted December,
> Too happy, happy brook,
> Thy bubblings ne'er remember
> Apollo's summer look. . . .

How the bubblings of a brook can be charged with a failure of memory for what happened last summer, when new water is perpetually coursing along its channel, will puzzle the reader. And when he reaches the end of the stanza he will be further misdirected:

> But with a sweet forgetting,
> They stay their crystal fretting,
> Never, never petting
> About the frozen time.

He will take *stay their crystal fretting* to mean 'stop worrying about being iced over', when what Keats really intended was 'they will stop trying to wear away the banks (another meaning of *fret*) with their clear waters'. The reader's eye will also be confused by the word *petting*, which here stands for 'being petulant' rather than, as now, 'treating with endearments'. So he will naturally translate the *would 'twere so with many a gentle girl and boy* as Keats's wish that they would abstain from petting parties about the frozen time; namely, the first half of January. And he will then continue in the same sense: 'But as it is, they all writhe at the thought of the illicit pleasures they enjoyed in summertime, when Apollo the Sun-god enabled them to pet in comfort beside the unfrozen brook.'

Keats really meant, I suppose: 'If only girls and boys could forget the joys of summer, instead of regretting them with such agony when winter comes!'

The last four lines are baffling:

> To know the change and feel it,
> When there is none to heal it,
> Nor numbèd sense to steal it,
>   Was never said in rhyme. . . .

How anyone can heal a change, or how any numbed sense can steal a change, I honestly do not know. . . . *Was never said in rhyme* is perfectly true: this stanza is a unique muddle.

Keats applies *happy* to tree and brook because they go along with Nature, and accept winter as a necessary lull; but why *too happy*, a suggestion that they will be overtaken by misery in Spring? Perhaps he means that gentle girls and boys are unnecessarily miserable because they fail to imitate tree and brook and, growing jealous of their power for forgetting, call them *too happy*? But this is not clearly stated; he has got tangled up with his rhyme sequence and fails to preserve the sense. The poem cannot, I fear, be repaired. Even if Keats had started:

> This drear-nighted December,
> O naked chestnut tree,
> Thy twigs will scarce remember
> Their green felicity . . .

he would have got into the same mess as before—the fact being that girls and boys are just as amorous in December as during the summer, and can always look forward, as the tree does, to the next springtime. The question of old age and waning passions is not touched upon here.

*

Quiller-Couch omits *The Eve of St Agnes*, and all the personal poems inspired by Isabella Jones, Keats's Muse, except the so-called 'Last Sonnet'—*Bright Star, Would I Were Steadfast As Thou Art*—which he had addressed to Isabella before he ever met Fanny Brawne. You can read about Isabella in Robert Gittings's recently published '*Keats: The Living Year*'. Most of you will recall that ecstatic midnight picnic in *The Eve of St Agnes*:

> Then by the bed-side, where the faded moon
> Made a dim, silver twilight, soft he set
> A table, and, half anguish'd, threw thereon
> A cloth of woven crimson, gold and jet:—
> O for some drowsy Morphean amulet!
> The boisterous, midnight, festive clarion,
> The kettle-drum, and far-heard clarinet,
> Affray his ears, though but in dying tone:—
> The hall door shuts again, and all the noise is gone.
>
> And still she slept an azure-lidded sleep,
> In blanched linen, smooth, and lavender'd,
> While he from forth the closet brought a heap
> Of candied apple, quince, and plum, and gourd;
> With jellies soother than the creamy curd,
> And lucent syrops, tinct with cinnamon;
> Manna and dates, in argosy transferr'd
> From Fez; and spicèd dainties every one,
> From silken Samarkand to cedar'd Lebanon.
>
> These delicates he heap'd with glowing hand
> On golden dishes and in baskets bright
> Of wreathèd silver: sumptuous they stand
> In the retired quiet of the night,
> Filling the chilly room with perfume light.—

'And now, my love, my seraph fair, awake!
'Thou art my heaven, and I thine eremite:
'Open thine eyes, for meek St Agnes' sake,
'Or I shall drowse beside thee, so my soul doth ache.'

This, as Robert Gittings shows, records Keats's midnight escapade with Isabella on St Agnes' Eve, January 20, 1819. The anachronistic long carpets rising along the gusty floor were laid in the love-nest lined for her at 34 Gloucester Street, Holborn, by the old bald-pate Donough O'Callaghan, M.P., her rich septuagenarian Whig protector. Isabella, later credited by Charles Woodhouse, Keats's friend, with having suggested the theme of the poem, was about Keats's own age. Her beauty, character, judgement and taste included her in the same remarkable company of *hetairai* as Harriet Wilson of the *Memoirs*— my favourite early nineteenth-century autobiographer— though, indeed, Harriet restricted her favours to the nobility.

Hush, hush! tread softly! hush, hush my dear!
  All the house is asleep, but we know very well
That the jealous, the jealous old bald-pate may hear,
  Tho' you've padded his night-cap—O sweet Isabel!
    Tho' your feet are more light than a Fairy's feet,
    Who dances on bubbles where brooklets meet,—
Hush, hush! soft tiptoe! hush, hush my dear!
For less than a nothing the jealous can hear.

No leaf doth tremble, no ripple is there
  On the river.—all's still, and the night's sleepy eye
Closes up, and forgets all its Lethean care,
  Charm'd to death by the drone of the humming Mayfly;
    And the Moon, whether prudish or complaisánt,
    Has fled to her bower, well knowing I want
No light in the dusk, no torch in the gloom,
But my Isabel's eyes, and her lips pulp'd with bloom.

Lift the latch! ah gently! ah tenderly—sweet!
We are dead if that latchet gives one little clink!
Well done—now those lips, and a flowery seat—
  The old man may sleep, and the planets may wink;
    The shut rose shall dream of our loves, and awake
    Full blown, and such warmth for the morning's take,
The stock-dove shall hatch her soft brace and shall coo,
While I kiss to the melody, aching all through!

Isabella had indeed padded O'Callaghan's night-cap: that is to say, had given him an overdose of what we now know was Ferintosh's famous Scotch Whisky; but the lovers would have been ruined had the latchet of the door given a single clink. The situation was an impossible one. Isabella, I think, loved Keats as wholeheartedly as she ever loved anyone: and he, her. But while she lived under the old bald-pate's protection, they could come together only on terms morally difficult for both. Marriage was out of the question; even if he had enjoyed better health. He had no money and no talents that could be harnessed to money-making. She was accustomed to a life of luxury and indolence, and had nothing to sell but her charms. Yet *The Eve of St Agnes* and *Bright Star* somehow insulate and make durable their true sense of each other, in a way that his subsequent infatuation with Fanny Brawne never did. Isabella was wise and generous. Fanny was a coquettish *Belle Dame Sans Merci*, who gave him little but pain.

*

Verse-craft, as practised in monumental masonic style, cannot admit the least 'fie-fie', as it was once called, or breach of polite convention. Thus Burns's stickily sentimental version of *John Anderson My Jo John* has long usurped the wonderfully vigorous original, printed at last in a collection called *The Merry Muse*; where the faithful wife deplores her husband's declining virility.

Burns comes off badly in the *Oxford Book of English Verse*. His was a difficult case. As an authentic ploughman and ribald satirist of low life, he had a wonderful sense of language. Take, for example, *The Holy Fair*, meaning the administration of the Sacrament, in a rowdy Scots parish:

> . . . Here farmers gash, in ridin' graith'
>   Gaed hoddin by their cottars;
> There, swankies young, in braw braid-claith,
>   Are springin' owre the gutters.
> The lasses, skelpin' barefit, thrang,
>   In silks and scarlets glitter;
> Wi' sweet-milk cheese, in mony a whang,
>   An' farlis bak'd wi' butter,
>   Fu' crump that day.

> . . . Here stands a shed to fend the show'rs
>   An' screen our country gentry,
> There, racer Jess, an' two-three whores,
>   Are blinkin' at the entry.
> Here sits a raw of tittlin' jauds,
>   Wi' heaving breast and bare neck,
> An' there a batch o' wabster lads,
>   Blackguarding frae Kilmarnock
>   For fun this day.

> Here some are thinkin' on their sins,
>   An' some upo' their claes;
> Ane curses feet that fyl'd his shins,
>   Anither sighs and prays:
> On this hand sits a chosen swatch,
>   Wi' screw'd-up grace-proud faces;
> On that a set o' chaps at watch,
>   Thrang winkin' on the lasses
>   To chairs that day.

... Now a' the congregation o'er
   Is silent expectation:
For Moodie speels the holy door,
   Wi' tidings o' damnation.
Should Hornie, as in ancient days,
   'Mang songs o' God present him,
The vera sight o' Moodie's face,
   To's ain het hame had sent him
          Wi' fright that day.

Hear how he clears the points o' faith
   Wi' rattling an' wi' thumpin'!
Now meekly calm, now wild in wrath,
   He's stampin' an' he's jumpin'!
His lengthen'd chin, his turn'd-up snout,
   His eldritch squeal and gestures,
Oh, how they fire the heart devout,
   Like cantharidian plasters,
          On sic a day!

Unfortunately, Quiller-Couch drew the line at dialect, and instead fobbed his readers off with the genteel Burns who had been taken up by carefully English-speaking Edinburgh society and who, as the new national bard-designate, was cannily giving them what they thought they wanted:

O were my Love yon lilac fair,
   Wi' purple blossoms to the spring,
And I a bird to shelter there,
   When wearied on my little wing;
How I wad mourn when it was torn
   By autumn wild and winter rude!
But I wad sing on wanton wing
   When youthfu' May its bloom renew'd.

O gin my Love were yon red rose
   That grows upon the castle wa',

And I mysel a drap o' dew,
   Into her bonnie breast to fa';
O there, beyond expression blest,
   I'd feast on beauty a' the night;
Seal'd on her silk-saft faulds to rest,
   Till fley'd awa' by Phoebus' light.

A song of this kind demands perfection in sound, form
and sense; Burns has taken no trouble over it. The first
lines of the two stanzas should be parallel:

     O were my Love yon lilac fair . . .

should be matched by:

     O were my Love yon red, red rose. . . .

Alternatively:

     O gin my Love were yon red rose . . .

should be matched by:

     O gin my Love yon lilac were. . . .

Moreover, Burns changes his rhyme scheme in the two
stanzas: with eleven rhymes in the first, and only eight
in the second. Nor are the lilac and the rose parallel.
One is a whole bush; the other a single flower. The rose
grows upon the castle wa'; but why on such an unlikely
spot, we are not told—perhaps Burns is seated on a well-
stuffed drawing-room sofa in Castle Street, Edinburgh,
and pointing up through the braw window-panes to the
Castle high aboon? Where the lilac grows, we are not
told. The fourth line of the first stanza ends in *little wing;*
the eighth, in *wanton wing.* Perhaps he meant to contrast
weary wing with *wanton wing,* but could not quite

85

manage it. . . . The notion that a bird could mourn the damage caused to the bare lilac branches by autumn gales is ridiculous, as Burns knows well. But the ladies sitting around him may well swoon at the conceit.

The first half of the second stanza is in irreproachable Scots style, but the second half has become fashionably romantic:

> O there, beyond expression blest . . .

two ugly *esses* that he would have been ashamed to admit into *The Holy Fair*.

> I'd feast on beauty a' the night
> Seal'd on her silk-saft faulds to rest . . .

a line that drags altogether too sensuously for a song.

> Till fley'd awa' by Pheobus' light. . . .

On consulting Burns's original, I find not only that Quiller-Couch has officiously reversed the order of the stanzas, but that the lines:

> O gin my Love were yon red rose
>   That grows upon the castle wa',
> And I mysel a drap o' dew,
>   Into her bonnie breast to fa' . . .

are not Burns's own. The genuine ballad from which he borrowed them concerned, it seems, the beautiful heiress of some Scottish earl, to whose hand the poet dangerously aspired—a meaning which has been smothered by Burns's introduction of the lilac; lilac being a fashionable shrub not yet imported into Scotland when the rose of love still grew on that castle wa'.

86

Till fley'd awa' by Phoebus' light—but with *morning* instead of *Phoebus*—belongs to the original.

*

On climbing from ordinary verse into the region of poetry, we sometimes come upon incoherences seemingly due to haste and lack of poetic control, as in Blake's *The Tyger*. Angels were thick on Blake's staircase: some divinely eloquent, some mouthing nonsense. *The Tyger* makes a tremendous impact on the reader of the *Oxford Book of English Verse*, especially after his tedious progress through the earlier 'numbers' of the eighteenth century.

> Tiger, tiger, burning bright
> In the forests of the night,
> What immortal hand or eye
> Could frame thy fearful symmetry?
>
> In what distant deeps or skies
> Burnt the fire of thine eyes?
> On what wings dare he aspire?
> What the hand dare seize the fire?
>
> And what shoulder and what art
> Could twist the sinews of thy heart?
> And, when thy heart began to beat,
> What dread hand and what dread feet?
>
> What the hammer? What the chain?
> In what furnace was thy brain?
> What the anvil? What dread grasp
> Dare its deadly terrors clasp?
>
> When the stars threw down their spears,
> And water'd heaven with their tears,
> Did He smile His work to see?
> Did He who made the lamb make thee?

> Tiger, tiger, burning bright
> In the forests of the night,
> What immortal hand or eye
> Dare frame thy fearful symmetry?

But all is not well here. The lines:

> On what wings dare he aspire?
> What the hand dare seize the fire?

make a sudden change in tense from the past tense, *Burnt the fire of thine eyes*, to the present. 'He dare' was good eighteenth-century English for 'he dares'; but not for 'he durst', nor for 'he dared'. And the tenses are confused again in the next stanza:

> In what furnace was thy brain?
>   . . . What dread grasp
> Dare its deadly terrors clasp?

Also, the third stanza makes no obvious sense:

> And what shoulder and what art
> Could twist the sinews of thy heart?
> And, when thy heart began to beat,
> What dread hand and what dread feet?

This last question is incomplete. Blake may be thinking of the building-up of the tiger's remaining anatomy, but does not say so. Instead he switches to the metaphor of the smith working with hammer and anvil, and we suspect that *feet* has come into the poem for the sake of the rhyme, when we read:

> What the hammer? What the chain?
> In what furnace was thy brain?
> What the anvil?

For the chain also seems introduced for the sake of the rhyme. Chains are used in measurement, but not in smithcraft.

> What dread grasp
> Dare its deadly terrors clasp?

The antecedent to *its* is *anvil;* but who has ever seen a smith clasp his anvil? And if Blake is referring to the brain in the furnace, smiths who use hammer and anvil also use tongs to remove their artifacts from the fire.

One can seldom trace exactly the origin of any poetic muddle. This happens to be an exception, since the *Rossetti Manuscript* supplies early drafts of several of Blake's poems, including *The Tyger*. We find that the question

> What dread hand and what dread feet?

is incomplete simply because Blake has struck out the following rather turgid lines:

> Could fetch it from the furnace deep
> And in thy horrid ribs dare steep—
> In the well of sanguine woe?
> In what clay and in what mould
> Have thy eyes of fury rolled?

This last question shows, at least, that Blake had a potter's craft in mind and suggests that he let *what dread feet* stand as a reference to the potter's habit of puddling clay with his toes; perhaps also to the smith's use of his feet for working the bellows.

> When the stars threw down their spears,
> And water'd heaven with their tears . . .

The stars are, I suppose, angels (as sometimes in the

Scriptures), but Blake has not made it clear whether they throw down their spears in bellicose mood, or whether they merely let them fall from their grasp in grief.

We have a right to know what he means, but suspend our doubts because of the clarity with which he asks:

> Did He smile His work to see?
> Did He who made the lamb make thee?

A simple omission of the middle part of the poem would repair the damage:

> Tiger, tiger, burning bright
> In the forests of the night,
> What immortal hand or eye
> Could frame thy fearful symmetry?
>
> In what distant deeps or skies
> Burnt the fire of thine eyes?
> On what wings dared he aspire?
> What the hand dared seize the fire?
>
> And what shoulder and what art
> Could twist the sinews of thy heart?
> Did He smile His work to see?
> Did He who made the lamb make thee?
>
> Tiger, tiger, burning bright
> In the forests of the night,
> What immortal hand or eye
> Dared frame thy fearful symmetry?

The truth is that Blake could not reconcile poetic creation, whether human or divine, with planned intellectual creation, or inspired human behaviour with moral laws; and it may be argued that the very confusion of his mind, when he considers the problem of how an All-loving God could have created both lamb and tiger, lends the poem this needed agonizing element. I cannot agree. If a poet believes wholly in what he says, the right words—however distraught they seem—will leap up to their exact place in the poem; and these are clearly not the right ones.

*

Coleridge's *The Ancient Mariner* is printed here at full length. It was first published in *Lyrical Ballads*, Coleridge's collaboration with Wordsworth; who persuaded him that any supernatural incidents of which he wrote should be put under the discipline of the natural emotions that they excited. This accounts for the extraordinary alternation of pure poetry and bathetic twaddle in *The Ancient Mariner*. The poem begins pseudo-dramatically with a wedding. The bridegroom's next-of-kin and, apparently, 'best man' is stopped at the church door by an old sailor who insists on telling him a long, irrelevant story—though why no one sends the rascal about his business, we are not told. And the poem ends moralistically with:

> 'Farewell, farewell! but this I tell
> To thee, thou Wedding-Guest!
> He prayeth well, who loveth well
> Both man and bird and beast.
>
> He prayeth best, who loveth best
> All things both great and small;
> For the dear God who loveth us,
> He made and loveth all.'
>
> The Mariner, whose eye is bright,
> Whose beard with age is hoar,
> Is gone: and now the Wedding-Guest
> Turn'd from the bridegroom's door.
>
> He went like one that hath been stunn'd,
> And is of sense forlorn:

> A sadder and a wiser man
> He rose the morrow morn.

In the middle of the poem we are subjected to an implausibly banal dialogue between two spirits, which begins:

> '"But tell me, tell me! speak again,
> Thy soft response renewing—
> What makes that ship drive on so fast?
> What *is* the Ocean doing?"'

And we are introduced to an unnecessary Hermit good who lives in a wood, Which slopes down to the sea; He loves to talk with mariners, Who come from a far countree. . . . But the rest of the poem is extraordinary, from a wholly other region; and though clumsy in places, beyond all textual criticism. As when the small sail-boat comes close up to the ship:

> And straight the Sun was fleck'd with bars
> (Heaven's Mother send us grace!)
> As if through a dungeon-grate he peer'd
> With broad and burning face.
>
> Alas (thought I, and my heart beat loud)
> How fast she nears and nears!
> Are those her sails that glance in the Sun,
> Like restless gossameres?
>
> Are those her ribs through which the Sun
> Did peer, as through a grate?
> And is that Woman all her crew?
> Is that a Death? and are there two?
> Is Death that Woman's mate?
>
> Her lips were red, her locks were free,
> Her locks were yellow as gold:
> Her skin was white as leprosy,

The Nightmare Life-in-Death was she,
Who thicks man's blood with cold.

The naked hulk alongside came,
And the twain were casting dice;
'The game is done! I've won! I've won!'
Quoth she, and whistled thrice. . . .

Soon after which, we are asked to welcome a contrastive return to the pietistic sanity of the kirk on the hill and the villagers flocking there in Sunday attire.

By the way: an obscure British officer in the early eighteenth-century Merchant Navy, by name Simon Hatry, had the extraordinary fortune to enter twice into English literature: first as the mate of the vessel that rescued Alexander Selkirk (Robinson Crusoe) from the island of Juan Fernandez; and then as Coleridge's Ancient Mariner. Hatry seems to have died in a Spanish prison. He shot the albatross with a musket, not a crossbow; and, curiously enough, was thereby trying to placate his crew, who thought the bird unlucky—because it was black instead of white.

Coleridge has plunged down deep into his own hell, and though the false antiqueness of the ballad style in which he writes may offend an ear attuned to the real Border Ballads, the story somehow rings true. The ancient mariner reminds Coleridge of the gigantic powers which a poet can command under the true poetic trance, and of their destructiveness when not directed by love. Yet the vision was so frightening that Coleridge could not face its implications in terms of creative love between man and woman—as he again shirked them in *Christabel*—but turned instead to a love of simple uncommitted creatures, the water-snakes:

Beyond the shadow of the ship,
I watch'd the water-snakes:

93

They moved in tracks of shining white,
And when they rear'd, the elfish light
Fell off in hoary flakes.

Within the shadow of the ship
I watch'd their rich attire:
Blue, glossy green, and velvet black,
They coil'd and swam; and every track
Was a flash of golden fire.

O happy living things! no tongue
Their beauty might declare:
A spring of love gush'd from my heart,
And I bless'd them unaware:
Sure my kind saint took pity on me,
And I bless'd them unaware.

And from the water-snakes he slid down to the petty idealism of Christian neighbourliness, and of *brown bread, white bread, And a cottage well thatched with straw.*

Christabel was a demoness, not his own true love; and his poem about her grows shoddier and shoddier as it proceeds. But at least Coleridge understood the poetic problem, even if he could not live with it and had, instead, to seek the dubious consolations of Hegelian philosophy.

Heaven help all poets who try to live with the problem! The curse that falls on them is that they are continually forced by their poetic demon into ecstatic regions which they fatally seek to identify with their own domestic life, though forming part of a different world altogether. Such experience, if recorded with absolute truth, is what survives, what blossoms, what becomes themselves when the poets are dead—whether or not they have subsequently reneged and settled for every-day reality. All but a very few have reneged, earlier or later in life—though continuing to practise the banausic craft of verse; which has been the subject of these three lectures.

Oxford Chair of Poetry 1965

LECTURE ONE

Lecture One, 1965

Throughout my lectures of the past four years I have dwelt on the difference between Muse Poetry and Apollonian poetry: a difference between the non-ecstatic and the ecstatic—*ecstasy* meaning in Greek a 'standing outside'. Outside what? I suppose outside the reality of our physical circumstances: so that any practical 'because' of a poem seems irrelevant to its nature.

In Muse poetry, the 'because' of a poem must be the poet's personal obsession with the Muse. Apollonian poetry is an arrangement of reasonable opinions in a memorizable verse form, with carefully chosen semi-archaic diction lending them authority: in fact, a form of rhetoric, which meets society's demand for the god of rational enlightenment rather than for the impractical Muse.

My views on the Muse Goddess are deduced from the multi-lingual corpus of love-poetry. I regard her as the primitive female who has separated herself from whatever laws have hitherto governed society, and whom man consistently fails to discipline. She is guardian of the love magic which all religious leaders, philosophers, and legalists in turn officiously attempt to define for her but which always eludes them. Only poets are convinced that a watchful trust in the undisciplined Muse Goddess will eventually teach them poetic wisdom and make them welcome to her secret paradise. Muse poetry is a distillation of love in its most unsocial, unphilosophical, unlegalistic, unliterary sense; written occasionally by those few women poets whom the Goddess possesses but, far more often, by men who have been granted access to her love-magic.

97

History begins with patriarchal annals:

> And each new year would recapitulate
> The unkind sloughings and renewals
> Of the death-serpent's chequered coat.

Poetic love is uncalendared, and a woman's capacity for Musedom cannot be measured by her ethical virtues, or by her intellectual powers, or by any of the qualities that make a good wife, mistress, secretary. The sole proof will be that the poet has responded to a magic of her own without which his poems would have remained sterile. He may be reproached for celebrating someone without constancy of direction, tenderness of conscience or recognized social background, rather than standing by a nobler, more predictable, other woman whose fixed devotion to duty should earn her the highest eulogies. But solid virtues, tempered by intellect and loyalty to social convention, yield no poetic inspiration; and who would reproach an electrical engineer for showing only vague interest in a huge lump of forty-percent copper ore, or even in a gold nugget, when what he really needed was rock containing minute but recoverable traces of uranium or titanium? The chemistry of poetic magic cannot be explained; it can only be observed. Magic originates with women, but is extended as a love-gift to man. The concealed purpose of modern university education for women is to drain off the magic. On the whole it is successful: but some women resist. Not many; just a few.

According to traditional religious dogma, the Goddess Bau, or the God Marduk, or Jehovah, or Prometheus, or Odomancona, or some other deity, created man from dust or clay. Palaeontologists dismiss this view as erroneous, arguing from fossilized bones that human beings have evolved from earlier creatures and that, though we have

98

been men or hominoids in the physical sense for some six million years or so, yet lizards and even lower forms of life must be acknowledged among our ancestors. Physically this is true; we are primates, close cousins of the ape, sloth, tarsier, lemur and loris. Yet we are separated even from the ape, our nearest-in-kin, by an immense gulf not so much of intelligence as of magic. Apes can be taught to roller-skate, smoke cigarettes and not disgrace themselves at a tea party; but little more.

At some point in prehistory, perhaps not more than a couple of hundred thousand years ago, perhaps even less, a man and a girl—as I conceive the scene—looked at each other in wonder under the full moon and signalled: 'We are we.' This birth of magic incidentally encouraged the fine arts of flint chipping, pottery, weaving and tattooing; but must have meant to these first real ancestors of ours far more than an expanded use of tools. It will have implied the discovery of such supernatural faculties as prophecy, healing, close communing at a distance, disembodied travel, and especially the magical extension of sexual understanding between man and woman into an all-powerful interchange of souls, for which lovers' gifts are the metaphor. These can be judged neither by their price nor by their utility, nor need they commemorate a particular anniversary. It is the surprise of their exact rightness and timing that distinguishes them from ordinary gifts. A shell, leaf, feather or curious stone carries an unspoken message clarifying the choice. As the author of the Elizabethan lutanist song *Fine Knacks for Ladies* wrote:

> Great gifts are guiles and look for gifts again;
> My trifles come as treasures from the mind.
> It is a precious jewel to be plain:
> Sometimes in shell the Orient's pearl we find.

The truth of love is proved by a constant change of such slight gifts, and imperilled by the greater ones—especially, of course, money, however useful in practical life.

Not improbably, however, the love-token custom was borrowed from the bower-bird and penguin, and love was lent a more domestic sense by observation of doves, ravens and storks, whose marital faithfulness as pairs had hitherto been unknown among primates. Wings have long emblemized freedom and exaltation; and the sensation of having the heart sprout feathers is a common phenomenon among lovers. On the other hand, the organization of clans and tribes for mutual defence or food sharing seems likely to have been borrowed from ants, bees and other insect communities, where individual love-pairing is unusual. The basic present dilemma of mankind is, indeed, whether we should go for wisdom to the ant, or to the dove. Flying dreams are prophetically indicative of the latter choice.

The bitter nineteenth-century conflict between priests and scientists as to the origin of man can be resolved by agreeing that Adam and Eve (or Deucalion and Pyrrha) were the first true man and woman, moulded suddenly by a divine impulse. A mother's natural control over her children until they fend for themselves sanctified matriarchy, a later stage in human development: the control being now extended into adult life. Male totem-clans gave their allegiance to a Queen Mother, who claimed not only descent from the Moon as a visible emblem and source of magic, but the magical monopoly of agriculture and arboriculture, in trust for her female kin. Matriarchy, however, put man in such awe of woman that it falsified the original love-union between Adam and Eve. Magic ceased to be a secret shared between lovers and became a royal female attribute used for tribal ends; and, finding monogamy irksome, matriarchal women took lovers only for as long as it suited them.

The 'heroic' age followed, poetic in part but cut short by a patriarchal revolution. Kings usurped power, claiming to be of solar descent; woman's mysteries were profaned, and women gradually degraded to drudges. The patriarchs ruled by force, reason and sorcery—sorcery being the male employment of magic for private ends—and by glorifying man as the superior sex. Judaism, Christianity and Islam set religious seals on this new dispensation.

Where are we now? Patriarchy still rules in theory; but the father no longer plays the domestic tyrant as he did throughout Old Testament times and still does in the Middle East. The Western world has accepted a mechanarchy which collectivizes human life—women's as much as men's. Financiers, politicians and scientists, relying on the people's traditional subservience to Queen-Mothers and Kings, have used the figment of democracy to seize power. In mythological terms it is another Palace Revolution of the Gods Hermes, Pluto and Apollo against Father Zeus; and except in old-fashioned monarchies and backward faiths allows no sacrosanct man or woman to prolong the illusion of divine magic. Allegiance to the State, a political machine with financial and scientific buttresses, is required instead. Everywhere the trend is towards a scientific and financial *élite* working closely with a political *élite*, to control and administer all human necessities, to reduce superstition—'superstition' meaning what is 'left over' from old habits of thought and eradicate—or suppress—all individualistic being. This is done either by censorship and imprisonment, as beyond the Iron Curtain; or by an increasingly close State control of education, industry and communication, as in the Western world.

William Whyte, a contemporary American scientist employed as a mouthpiece of business corporations, explains their final object as social unanimity brought about

101

by reducing haphazard custom to terms of reason:

> The conditions which determine human happiness are discoverable scientific methods and largely capable of realization. The world's greatest need is a science of human relationship and an art of human engineering based on its laws. These relationships are extremely complex, but science is gradually reducing them to fundamentals that respond to direct and simple treatment.

William Whyte is claiming that one can eventually fool not only half the people all the time, nor all the people half the time, but all the people all the time. And Elton Mayo, founder of the Harvard School of Business and the 'human relations' school of industrial psychology, envisages a happy collectivism on the lines of the Australian aboriginal societies:

> . . . an almost perfect collaboration drilled into members of a tribe in such a fashion that a kinship relation, a social ceremony, or an economic duty, become signals or commands to act or respond in a certain manner—each member knows his place and part, although he cannot explain it. A century of scientific development and the effects of education have led us to forget how necessary this type of non-logical social action is to satisfactory achievement in living.

It is true that the few aboriginal tribes still not wholly contaminated by missionaries or traders live an almost insectival life—in automatic obedience to tribal custom even where the individual seems penalized because the due rewards of his skill are denied him. But at least they use their bodies and senses to the full, in their successful survival of climatic hardships which would destroy any unequipped modern man within a week. What Elton Mayo demands is instinctive obedience to a political machine, controlled by logical experts who will gladly employ direct or indirect brainwashing techniques to secure non-logical allegiance.

We are still living in the Late Christian Age among superstitious relics of even earlier cultures, but there can be no doubt what is being planned for us. We are to be insects, not birds. The new mechanarchic ideal is to free peoples not only from the need to think for themselves, but from the temptation to form habits inconsistent with the smooth development of rational life. The justificatory excuse is that no violence must imperil the mechanarchic ant-heap, and that reduced working hours should allow ants as much leisure time as possible for private amusement. Yet the financial and political importance of this leisure time, which already amounts to three-quarters of every human week, has been carefully assessed. Our would-be rulers are set on so controlling leisure-time that the mainly mechanized entertainment provided will hypnotize us into also accepting their inescapably mechanized employment. Modern finance has become a careful card-castle of organized endless debt, in which workers are involved by the hire-purchase system, by compulsory insurance, by inflation of currency, by taxation that discourages savings, and by constant temptations to spend the last penny they owe.

The countryside is industrialized. Horses are supplanted by tractors, the soil is poisoned by chemicals and wild life exterminated; farmers are told what to plant and how much; farm labourers, directed into industry, bequeath their cottages as week-end pleasances for the richer townsfolk. Picturesque villages become holiday centres with urban business controlling all rustic amenities: village bakeries are disappearing; village breweries have long disappeared; little of the food locally eaten originates locally; saddlers, thatchers, smiths, carpenters and even masons grow rare.

Since few except the aged take religion seriously, the

103

parish priest has become a welfare officer rather than a saver of souls. Unless professing himself a modernist—or even in extreme cases an agnostic—and adapting himself to the mechanarchic process, he can exercise almost no ethical authority. Yet, since business encourages a religious façade, births, marriages and deaths are still largely solemnized under ecclesiastic authority—as business also converts the trappings of constitutional monarchy into a tourist attraction, and protects the ancient sanctity of gold by keeping the gold-standard alive while withdrawing gold coin from circulation.

Oliver Goldsmith wrote nostalgically in 1769:

> How often have I bless'd the coming day,
> When toil, remitting, lent its turn to play,
> And all the village train, from labour free,
> Led up their sports beneath the spreading tree.

Sport has long left the village green and become professionalized. Intensive training for particular events breaks new athletic records every year; modern football, scientifically played, is watched by enormous crowds, few of whom have ever played themselves, and has become the roulette table for vast betting schemes. This limited development of individuals fails to remedy the general physical inertia; for although stuffy and crowded dance-halls may limber up a good number of restless teenagers there is little demand for new playing-fields.

Has mankind ceased to think creatively and abdicated in favour of a self-perpetuating mechanical process, automatically geared to public education? Fifty years ago only one American citizen in twenty went to college; now fourteen do so. The proportion is also rising steeply in the United Kingdom; universities are proliferating. Everyone seems much happier because everyone shares the same worries. Most businessmen, scientists, educationalists and executives claim to have clean consciences besides occasional ulcers and cardiac weaknesses. They prefer to assume that the mechanarchic system is under control, with careful economic and scientific safeguards against collapse. All ugly phenomena are swept under the rug every morning. The fact is that no dictator with an anthropological bent has yet been summoned to take even nominal charge of the mechanarchic process. Indeed, nobody at all is in charge, and individual experts in this science or that have very poor liaison with one another. Even worse liaison exists between national blocs, despite international conferences and the boasted advance of scientific reasoning.

What has become of magic? Does its denial by the mechanarchs imply its reversion to the first discoverers of love-miracle: to a reborn Eve and Adam? Since all social virtues are now associated with complicity in the antimagical State, Eve is likely to have had 'a difficult home background' where patriarchal control has broken down. She will be passionately proud of her womanhood and of her latent powers: ready to bestow love, but unwilling to risk humiliation at the hands of any would-be husband, and wildly shying away from the least threat of male possessiveness. *'Adam, Adam, ubi es?'* she cries, and is seldom answered except by Samael the subtle serpent.

Adam is equally disappointed in his search for Eve. Catullus' 'Lesbia'—if Apuleius was right in identifying her with Clodia, second daughter of Publius Claudius Pulcher, Cicero's enemy—came from one of the most difficult home backgrounds in Rome, a family notorious for incest and sacrilege. Catullus may have read her wildness not as viciousness (which it seems to have been) but as wholesome criticism of a social morality no longer based on faith in the divine. Living in spirit outside the dead world which such wild women also reject, a poet trusts them to use their magic for poetic, curative and creative ends. He looks both backwards and forwards to the appearance of miracle in regions exempt from contumaceous male philosophy. Wild women do indeed recognize the part which they are thus expected to play, and the creation of poetic magic can be a prospect that entrances them. Yet, even when the bond of physical love is transcended by magical experience, they still suspect its threat to their freedom of action. Too often they dismiss their poets, resenting that love-magic cannot be wholly divorced from the physical love, not in itself sacramental, which Adam and Eve enjoyed in Eden. Zoologically, poets and wild women are still primates.

Desire first, by a natural miracle
United bodies, united hearts, blazed beauty;
Transcended bodies, transcended hearts.

Two souls, now unalterably one
In whole love always and for ever,
Soar out of twilight, through upper air,
Let fall their sensuous burden.

Is it kind, though, is it honest, even,
To consort with none but spirits—
Leaving true-wedded hearts like ours
In enforced night-long separation
Each to its random bodily inclination,
The thread of miracle snapped.

The question of faith kept between a poet and his incarnate Muse is legally unresolvable. Catullus wrote bitterly:

Caeli, Lesbia nostra, Lesbia illa,
illa Lesbia, quam Catullus unam
plusquam se atque suos amavit omnes,
nunc in quadriviis et angiportis
glubit magnanimi Remi nepotes.

And when the thread snaps, poems alone, for what they are worth, survive to record its suprahuman moments.

Now that contraceptive devices provide one main mechanarchic solution of the leisure-time problems, and now that the publishing of sexological literature has been approved by our courts of Justice, few young women still feel bound to hoard their virginity for future husbands. The prevailing custom is, as among Polynesians, to experiment with a sequence of lovers. Yet it goes against a poet's nature to sleep with anyone but the women with whom he is in love: mere physical congress spells for him a loss of virtue—virtue in the sense of power. The New Testament Greek word for what Jesus felt stolen from him when secretly touched by a woman patient is *dynamis*, power; and though in that case the loss of virtue was ritual rather than poetic—the woman suffered from vaginal hæmorrhage and her touch would have made him unclean for some hours—the principle remains the same. A poet feels unclean when his body has betrayed him, and finds *sex* a dirty word: it implies an adulterated public view of a private ritual between two individuals. A Muse woman feels the same: although her sense of honour is not a male one, she never plays her body false. While gratified by the poet's attachment and humorously jealous of rivals, she may well become irked by his intensity and prefer another man's undemanding casualness; for monogamy is a patriarchal, not a matriarchal, invention. If a Muse-woman should feel a natural need for children, her poet may well seem the most unsuitable possible choice as a husband: his physical faithfulness threatening her emotional independence. Even while admitting herself inevitably bound to him as the one man who has fully recognized her powers, she may argue that his passionately declared love is essentially self-esteem, that his tears are tears of self-pity, and that the poems which she inspires and for which he gets the credit are in a sense stolen from her. Why not choose a simple, uncomplicated, wholly unpoetic husband? How could the poet deny her that pleasure?

The mythical role allotted to the White Goddess reflects much the same situation. She is represented as making alternate love first to the creative, impassioned demi-God of the Waxing Year, and then in pity to his murderer, the luckless demi-God of the Waning year, named Lack, Drought and Envy.

A poet cannot afford to identify himself with any organization formed for political, financial or ecclesiastic ends. There is no fixed rule for his social behaviour except to be himself and live in the company of those like-minded. At the outbreak of the First World War I volunteered for the regular infantry and found myself among men whom detestable trench conditions and persistent danger either destroyed or ennobled. Although we were caught in a demonic machine, officially sanctified by a corps of regular padres; although the war's final result would be worse than the power-politics that had caused it, ordinary civilized virtues had given place to heroic ones. We remained free because we were volunteers and bound to one another by a suicidal sacrament. Holding a trench to the last round of amunition and the last man, taking a one-in-three chance of life when rescuing a badly wounded comrade from no-man's-land, keeping up a defiant pride in our soldierly appearance: these were poetic virtues. Our reward lay in their practice, with possible survival as a small bright light seen at the end of a long tunnel. We despised all civilians; wounds were nothing by comparison with the grief of losing new-found friends in the periodic massacres. Yet after only a few weeks of trench life in a dangerous sector we grew sick, poisoned by our own adrenal glands, our memories became impaired and the sense of crisis grew less intense; it took some of us as long as ten years to recover our health.

Though most of my comrades were content, after the War, to relax, find a safe job, marry 'the only girl in the world', and become respectable members of the British Legion, I swore a poetic oath never again to be anyone's servant but my own; and gradually grew more and more obsessed by poetic principle. Its sorrows and distresses proved in their way as acute as my war-time ones.

The pride of 'bearing it out even to the edge of doom' that sustains a soldier in the field, governs a poet's service to the Muse. It is not masochism, or even stupidity, but a determination that the story shall end gloriously: a willingness to risk all wounds and hardships, to die weapon in hand. For a poet this defiance is, of course, metaphorical: death means giving in to dead forces, dead routines of action and thought. The Muse represents eternal life and the sudden lightning-flash of wisdom.

The walking dead surround the poetic obsessionist, trying to interest him in universal topicality, and at the same time to drain his life-force. 'The world must go on,' they tell him. 'Why not join us? Support the machine that we have created, and give it an appearance of human meaning. Join our guild of united morticians. We will pay you well and shower honours on you—you may even be elected an honorary vice-president.'

'You smell like the dead,' he answers. 'Give me the faintest proof that you still have any spark of life left in you, and I will listen.'

No answer.

He is tempted to use violence on them, in the hope of awakening some faint living response. But it is unlucky to strike the dead; and if he does so, the worst they can do is to send him a lawyer's letter of complaint. And a poet cannot live always at the pinnacle of his power, among the similarly entranced: he needs simple, virtuous, lively neighbours with whom he can watch the clouds go by.

*

109

Richard Korn, an American poet, enlarges bitterly on those ugly phenomena swept under the rug every morning: especially by organizations which the State sponsors for keeping its underprivileged, sick or deliquent citizens in order. He writes that the novice who chooses to work in one of these 'Human Service bureaucracies' brings with him little more than his training qualifications, his enthusiasm and a reflected faith that the Human Service can redeem the lost, sick or needy committed to its charge; but his passage from the stage of novice to that of professional is chequered by shocks and disillusions. Only his poker-faced acceptance of these will mark him in his colleagues' eyes as fully matured. The earliest and bitterest disillusion is the discovery that his particular Human Service cannot possibly fulfil the mission assigned to it: that crime, mental disease or poverty need national solutions. If he enquires why his colleagues have not yet forced these problems on the public, he meets with a second major disillusion. They are all, he finds, aware of their own ineffectuality but unanimous on the need for public confidence in Human Services. He learns the great unwritten law of bureaucracy: 'Do Nothing to Embarrass Us'. Every bureaucracy lives in a perpetual state of fear that public knowledge of its inadequacies may lead to disenfranchisement; so that an inordinate amount of effort is wasted in dishonestly maintaining a favourable public image. Staff-members aware of organizational felonies must be silenced, and the best technique is to involve them in complicity; thus no member can be promoted until he has demonstrated his readiness to betray the community on behalf of the organization.

The novice's third shock is the discovery that no bureaucracy can survive except by shelving the very responsibilities that it was created to accept. The policeman must live with a guilty awareness that the largest single class of persons systematically and daily violating the law are his fellow-policemen. The mental-health worker must accept the fact that the largest single class of persons engaged in the mistreatment of the mentally sick are his fellow-workers at the hospital. And so on. If he is willing to sacrifice his personal scruples for the up-keep of the organization he will even perhaps be decora-ted as a public benefactor. If he chooses to serve the community in disregard of the organization's *amour propre*, he will be defined as a traitor and probably expelled from his profession. If he elects to remain, avoiding what complicity he can in official misdemean-ours, he may be tolerated so long as his good works do not obstruct the organization's most pressing business: that of self-aggrandizement. But, in such cases, he must content himself with permament low status under constant threat of expulsion. If he fights the system and denounces it, he will die in good company—with the philosopher Alexander Herzen who thus diagnosed his intellectual generation: 'We are not the doctors. We are the disease.'

Richard Korn's picture may be overdrawn, and he is writing about his own country, not ours. But the bureaucratic spirit is international. My own decision to remain free after leaving the Army was caused in part by having found myself forced into complicity with military misdemeanour, as an officer of sufficient rank to sit on courts-martial. Once when ordered by the Divisional General to pronounce sentence of death on a deserter, in aid of military morale, I did wrong. Instead of attending the court-martial and boldly protesting against this iniquitous order I made an exchange with the only other competent officer available: he attended the court-martial while I took over his command in the trenches.

Some would-be poets expect the State to support them. So do artists. I sympathize more with the artists, because they get a far rougher deal: from the art-dealers who

111

decide on trends, prices and personality cults. An artist who fails to do what his Gallery expects of him may have no means of paying for his rent and materials. But the sort of artist whom a bureaucracy would choose to hire is rarely one whose pictures I should choose for my own walls. The poet needs no materials except pen and ink, and his task is, or should be, to remove himself from the State's line of vision. He knows his powerlessness to effect any immediate betterment of society; but he can at least keep the flame of magic alight among his few intimates.

Until a hundred years ago, a small liberal-minded section of the community, sponsored by some eccentric millionaire, could produce a local working-model for a better world. That time has passed. 'It just won't work, Mac,' as I heard early this year at the Green Hornet Bar in Greenwich Village, New York, where a wild Boston Irishman edged up to me and began talking about millions of poor devils starving in India and Africa and China and such places; and about the thousands of gangsters and delinquents in the big cities; and about the hundreds of Federal ships tied up empty in the Hudson, waiting for God only knew what.

'I'm a stranger here,' I said cautiously. 'A Limey. But you may be right. There's always marginal tonnage lying around except in war-time. When the freight rates rise, it can amount to a lot.'

He went on about the huge farm surpluses that Americans either hoard or destroy, because nobody there can eat it all, and because the poor starving devils abroad can't pay for it all: and about the vast criminal waste in New York and the other big cities—enough to feed and clothe millions! And about all those philanthropic Christian and Jewish do-gooders and Peace Corps characters who want to prevent crime, starvation, idleness.

The barman said: 'What the hell, Mac? All this don't hurt *you* none, surely?'

112

Mac said: 'Sure, it hurts me as a human being. I ask myself: why can't we put the Christian and Jewish do-gooders in charge of the delinquent no-gooders? Why not give the no-gooders a grand job which would be to load those idle boats (or "marginal tonnage", as the Prof. calls them) with surplus food and clothing and send them sailing over the wide ocean with gifts for the poor starving devils abroad? Sure then everyone would feel good. What's wrong with that for a solution?'

'No, Mac,' said the barman. 'It just wouldn't work. The Longshoremen's Union and the Seamen's Union and the Teamsters Union would raise hell. And you've got to respect Big Business. Big Business wouldn't stand for any of that, not even to save the world from Communism—no more than the Unions wouldn't. Free gifts destroy markets, don't you see?'

Mac pointed out that there was no market there, anyway. He said: 'Those poor devils have no cash, so they have to starve. Only pump them up with cash and they'll start producing again and have money to throw around.'

'And put us Americans out of jobs by undercutting prices?' sneered the barman. 'No, Mac, it just wouldn't work. Forget it.'

I agreed that nothing sensible and simple ever works: just because no organizations *think* sensibly or simply. In the end, of course, something snaps and then you have a recession, or a war, which changes the problem.

*

What the Spaniards call a *duende* (short for *duen de la casa*—'master of the house') was originally a goblin or genie or, at the worst, a poltergeist that had taken possession of a home. It then came to mean the spirit that possesses dancers or singers at a house of entertainment

113

and makes them exceed their normal powers. The *duende* is caused by an exchange of love between performer and audience, unhindered by any inimical presence. Yet the word *duende* can be extended to the possession that makes poets, painters, and composers surpass themselves when working alone, animated by this magical love. This *duende* implies two complementary love-principles; one concerned with doing, the other with being: neither of which deserves separate credit for the product. Love is catching, like fire, wherever there is tinder. At a house of entertainment, although the *duende* seems to be born from a sudden recognition of complementary love between the main performer and a single member of the audience, it affects everyone present. One can readily distinguish the gasp of wonder when this sort of *duende* appears, from the loud applause that a footlight favourite can count upon, night after night, so long as the house is full, expectation high, and the seats expensive enough.

The miracle of true love—the *duende* that heals and enlightens any company into which a fortunate pair of lovers strays—is not rare. Yet few adults still recall those mystical visions of early childhood, first noted by the poet Vaughan, which correspond with their later intimations of love. The remainder either suppress them under pressure of practical logic; or surrender to comfortable routines of affection that keep love at a low simmer; or forfeit their powers by deliberate acts of cruelty, perversion or greed; or reject love as a social impossibility, choosing a second-best or third-best to fill the gap.

Ideally women *are*, meaning that they possess innate magic; sometimes they also *do*, but theirs is not doing in the male sense. Whenever men achieve something magically apt and right and surprising, their *duende* has always it seems been inspired by women. Whatever they attempt in male pride, by the ingenious use of intellect or fancy, is sorcery rather than magic.

114

Woman with her forests, moons, flowers, waters,
And watchful fingers:
We claim no magic comparable to hers—
At best, poets; at worst, sorcerers.

Right doing by men is achievement. Right doing by woman is a simple by-product of being; quiet, unemphatic, non-competitive, breath-taking.

Most ordinary couples are ripe for constant bickering even before their honeymoon has ended, with concealed jealousies and resentments leading to open fights, and open fights leading to passionate reconciliations. They argue that since marriage limits sexual freedom, any violent marital quarrel with its happy ending of renewed mutual embraces will prove that love is still alive—and not merely in the domestic sense which implies a common purse, routine planning, shared meals, regular hygienic love-making and the careful maintenance of children. But bickering can grow ugly. The time comes when quarrels find no passionate sequel of forgiveness, but only sullen brooding on vengeance or escape. Granted, in most bourgeois societies, amicable agreements allow both parties equal freedom of sexual unfaithfulness, though with careful safeguards to protect the social sanctity of marriage. Yet this implies affection and no longer love. True love may be presumed even after years of marriage; but how can a *duende* appear once a home has become a mere machine for living? It must at least be a centre where other lovers come calling with their excitements, troubles, and discoveries. And if the married pair can, by some miracle, preserve each other's freedom of action, avoiding any drudgery of planned routine, neither face need fail to light up at the sight of the other's after the briefest absence. But how many such pairs exist?

The obvious advantages of a home are that it allows

115

the exercise of unstinted hospitality, and the right to shut the front door fast against all that is idle, weak, sick, greedy or unreal. A single man or woman finds it harder to keep these elements away, because of loneliness. And yet most homes are prisons. Light a fire with the logs laid on a heap of kindling, the ends pointing into the room. It burns well; but the heap of kindling, namely shared meals and a shared double-bed, is soon consumed. Children grow up and lose close contact with their parents; and the fire of love goes out if the logs are placed either so closely together that no draught can pass between them, or so far apart that the space cannot be filled with the flame of truth.

A young man finds it difficult to realize that a woman is subject to two severe climactic changes from which he is exempt; motherhood and the menopause. He may even be unaware of her emotional rhythm while she is still subject to her monthly courses. And she finds it difficult to accept his inability to change as she changes. The case is complicated by the newly discovered male rhythm of emotional intensity, which does not coincide with the month and appears to be considerably longer than a woman's. And the man who experiences no dramatic change of life but, apart from a gradual slowing down of physical energies and a weakening of his vision, should remain substantially the same from the age of fifteen to seventy-five or longer. Usual mistakes on the woman's part are expecting him either to grow old gracefully before his time, or to remain young beyond his time—for many men are played out by forty.

Love is the main theme and origin of true poems. I have myself conceived it in quiet, elegiac terms: as of a golden wedding already celebrated in two hearts thrust through by the same golden dart; a life seasonally punctured by the feasts of Candlemas, when the country year begins; Midsummer, when nights are shortest; Martin-

116

mas, when Autumn reaches its peak; Christmas, the
family feast. Yet I found myself writing, very many
years ago during my first marriage:

Be assured, the Dragon is not dead
But once more from the pools of peace
Shall rear his fabulous green head.

The flowers of innocence shall cease
And like a harp the wind shall roar
And the clouds shake an angry fleece.

'Here, here is certitude,' you swore,
'Below this lightning-blasted tree.
Where once it struck, it strikes no more.

'Two lovers in one house agree.
The roof is tight, the walls unshaken.
As now, so must it always be.'

Such prophecies of joy awaken
The toad who dreams away the past
Under your hearth-stone, light forsaken,

Who knows that certitude at last
Must melt away in vanity—
No gate is fast, no door is fast—

That thunder bursts from the blue sky,
That gardens of the mind fall waste,
That fountains of the heart run dry.

Despite the elegiac 'true love' concept of domesticity,
to which my poems have returned time after time, I am
drawn to the conclusion that though a poet must experience this before understanding the full perils of his profession, there can be no solution in time, to the problem
of love; only in timelessness.

117

Blake speaks of 'the marriage-hearse', but it need be no hearse unless a poet expects from his wife more than tenderness, loyalty and affection. To marry the woman in whom the Muse is resident negates poetic principle; if only because the outward view of marriage implies wifely subservience to a husband. Recognition of magic on the poetic level is irreconcilable with the routine of domesticity; and once a woman's single love for a man has been distracted by love for her children, the magic tie between them breaks, however proud he may be of his fatherhood; if only because she must accept her social dependence on him. For me, poetry implies a courtship of the Muse prolonged into a magical principle of living. There is no domestic poetry.

Occasional married pairs come so close together in their shared routine as to enjoy only the same foods, drinks, music, pictures and plays; even their handwriting becomes almost identical. The Greeks knew them as 'Baucis and Philemon'; the English say 'Darby and Joan'. The one who dies first is not long survived by the other. Such identical love justified the institution of marriage for those worthy of it; their occasional bickering is playful, and for the most part used to assure the outside world that each retains personal liberty. Most ordinary married pairs air their painful disagreements only in private.

Complementary love, as distinct from the identical love of Darby and Joan, is the most difficult sort. Darby and Joan send each other such simple telepathic messages as: 'We must get the washing in; it will soon rain,' whereas those exchanged by complementary lovers are surprising to both.

> Lovers in time of absence need not signal
> With call and answering call:
> By sleight of providence each sends the other
> A clear more than coincidental answer

118

To every still unformulated puzzle,
Or a smile at a joke harboured, not yet made,
Or power to be already wise and unafraid.

The theme of complementary love does not occur in
Classical literature, even in Homer. Although the Siege
of Troy is provoked by Helen's fateful elopement with
Paris, the physical attraction between this pair is all that
we are allowed to see, and she calls herself a bitch for
having deserted her husband Menelaus and caused so
many deaths. The domestic affection between Hector and
his wife Andromache is endangered only by the sense of
male honour which sends him to his death at Achilles'
hands; but the blind overwhelming power which took
Helen to Troy has been sanctified in poetry at the ex-
pense of all other emotions, despite the eventual defeat of
both lovers.

What if Prince Paris, after taking thought,
Had not adjudged the apple to Aphrodite
But, instead, had favoured buxom Hera,
Divine defendress of the marriage couch?
What if Queen Helen had been left to squander
Her beauty upon the thralls of Menelaus,
Hector to die unhonoured in his bed,
Penthesileia to hunt a poorer quarry
The bards to celebrate a meaner siege?
Could we still have found the courage, you and I,
To embark together for Cranaë
And consummate our no less fateful love?

Apart from certain passages in the Song of Solomon
which Pharisee editors included in the Biblical canon
because of its traditional use at weddings, and because the
love of Solomon for the Shunemite could be used as a
metaphor of God's love for Israel, no word about complementary love is to be found in the Bible. Jacob's

119

readiness to serve seven years for Rachel, Laban's younger daughter, after already serving seven for Leah, should be read as a mythical anecdote explaining the predominance of the three Rachel tribes in Israel, although they were junior in origin to the Leah tribes. Even the attempt on Joseph by Potiphar's wife is not a love story; Joseph had no yearning for her and the Hebrew text makes it clear that Potiphar was a eunuch and that Zuleika, which was her name, would have dared anything to get herself with child.

Nevertheless the prime ancient legend concerned with poetic love is of Biblical origin: that of Solomon and the Queen of Sheba. Jewish, Arabic, Christian and Ethiopian sources show that its strength lay in the complementary nature of their bond; each having a crown to wear and neither being able to relinquish it for the other's sake.

A hundred questions about love stem from their story. The Queen of Sheba, it appears, came from a matriarchal, or at least a matrilineal, people, and will have had no husband, but only a subservient stud of lovers, representatives of the tribes owing her allegiance. The concept of a man living independently of his mother and grandmother, or of the woman who had chosen him as a semipermanent lover, must have been bizarre to her. Solomon, on the other hand, was a patriarch who inherited his father David's harem and added to it by marriage with princesses from the twelve tribes of Israel and from neighbouring royal houses; hence the matriarchal way of thinking, natural to the Queen of Sheba, must have astounded him.

They fell in complementary love; he never having met a real woman before, nor she a real man. No solution seemed possible: Solomon could not sail off for Sheba and there humble himself by becoming one more lover to the Queen; nor could she stay in Israel and humble herself by becoming merely one more of Solomon's wives or concubines. Nevertheless, she had a child by him, and according to some accounts they jointly conquered a new Ethiopian territory lying between their own countries, and placed the child, by name Menelik, on its throne; both would then visit its capital at the same time each year, and so renew their acquaintance.

True love is often discovered after one of the lovers, or both, has become involved in marriage, or taken a religious vow, or become otherwise inaccessible. Each is tempted to accuse the other of not sacrificing everything in their single cause. The *duende* instead of assisting their efforts to time a concerted flight in each other's company, becomes a dangerous poltergeist that causes physical sickness and accidents. It is better not to dwell on this, but rather on the wisdom that Solomon learned from his Queen.

LECTURE TWO

Lecture Two, 1965

A poet's life is ruled by the principle of avoiding loveless circumstance, or of passing through it as speedily and un-involvedly as possible. 'Loveless circumstance' means the full impress of mechanarchy, functionalism, routine: methods invented by scientists and financiers to de-humanize and control life. One can now, if it pleases, live entirely alone in a crowded city without speaking to a soul for weeks: mechanized transport, self-service supermarkets, self-service restaurants, built-in television entertainment, all-electric domestic service—(if one has the money)—and at the same time manage without any hand-made utensil, appliance or decoration whatsoever. This is the way of death, against which modern beat-poets inarticulately howl, while at the same time using language as a self-service contrivance to which they give a despairing twist or kick to show their disrespect for tradition. It never occurs to them that they can simply quit, walk away and go on walking until they come to a place where people are still dependent on one another for exchange of human warmth and services.

'Functionalism' is used by architects and industrial designers as a word of praise for the simplest and most economical design possible that will serve a single limited purpose. An atomic engineer from New Zealand once teased me for spending a lot of money on eighteenth-century silver spoons made by Hester Bateman, and on early nineteenth-century flint-glass tumblers—when I could have bought perfectly good functional table ware from Woolworth's at a twentieth of the price. Why pay for art and age? he asked. Had he been a simple financier

125

I should have explained that both the glass and silver would enhance their value at least 800% in the course of the next twenty years, if I took good care of them. But since he was a scientist I explained that he had forgotten a principle function of tableware: not only must it be of convenient size, weight and design for eating or drinking purposes, but it must encourage the appetite and create no fatigue-reaction. Polished silver and transparent glass, whatever their contents, stimulate the gastric juices; and the subtle differences in shape between each of a dozen hand-forged spoons or a dozen hand-blown tumblers, even if unengraved, give every place at table an individual look. Which (I added) is partly why restaurant meals seldom taste so good as those served in a well-furnished home, and why diners-out constantly try new places. Manufactured tableware is *dead*, like the interior decoration of most restaurants.

Functionalism in prose is a Latin concept, adapted by the French to their less rigid vernacular: the theory that ideas are inacceptable unless cast in certain set grammatic and vocabularistic forms. Neither Latin nor French has, of course, a purely mechanical flow; some words are more charged with emotion than others, and a stylist takes care to vary the rhythm of his paragraphs. Nevertheless, a grammarian in either language has the right to blue-pencil any sentence as incorrect. English prose, on the other hand, reserves for itself perfect freedom of idiosyncratic usage, and so while still able to convey subtle shades of meaning untranslatable into French or even Humanistic Latin need never weary the reader's eye. English-speaking scientists fall between two stools. They should never have discarded Humanistic Latin but, having done so, ought now to learn a live English that causes the reader no fatigue reactions.

My friend the late Norbert Wiener, Professor of Mathematics at the Massachusetts Institute of Technology, and an outstanding scientist, prefaces his famous book on Cybernetics with the following two paragraphs. He is trying to write simply in justification of the book's title: *The Human Use of Human Beings*. But although an electronic scientist, he has failed to respect the human brain as an electronic receiving apparatus which must be fed information in clear, accurate and unrepetitive style, never interrupted by atmospherics, 'fading effect', interference from other transmitters, or short circuits.

The beginning of the twentieth century marked more than the end of a hundred-year period and the start of another. There was a real change of point of view even before we made the political transition from the century on the whole dominated by peace, to the half century of war through which we have just been living. This was perhaps first apparent in science, although it is quite possible that whatever has affected science led independently to the marked break which we find between the arts and literature of the nineteenth and those of the twentieth centuries.

Newtonian physics, which had ruled from the end of the seventeenth century to the end of the nineteenth with scarcely an opposing voice, described a universe in which everything happened precisely according to law, a compact, tightly organized universe in which the whole future depends strictly upon the whole past. Such a picture can never be either fully justified or fully rejected experimentally and belongs in large measure to a conception of the world which is supplementary to experiment but in some ways more universal than anything that can be experimentally verified. We can never test by our imperfect experiments whether one set of physical laws or another can be verified down to the last decimal. The Newtonian view, however, was compelled to state and formulate physics as if it were, in fact, subject to such laws. This is now no longer the dominating attitude of physics, and the men who contributed most to its downfall were Bolzmann in Germany and Gibbs in the United States.

What he meant to write was, I think, something like this:

127

When the warlike twentieth century succeeded the pacific late-nineteenth, Western art, literature and politics were swiftly transformed; which seemed to justify the popular superstition that new centuries inaugurate new epochs of thought and sentiment. Perhaps the most striking change occurred in physics: Bolzmann in Germany and Gibbs in the United States together prompted a general rejection of Sir Isaac Newton's still dominant theory that the Universe is ruled by temporal causality. Though he had admitted his concept to be unverifiable by detailed experiment, because scientists can have only a limited view of the Universe—as we now admit it undisprovable for the same reason—Newton nevertheless framed what these two physicists considered altogether arbitrary laws for its presentation.

By omitting the suggestion in the first sentence of a popular century-superstition, on the general truth of which he fails to comment, and which is therefore irrelevant to his argument, Wiener could have reduced three hundred words to just over one hundred, and guarded his readers still further against fatigue. The principles of prose-writing underlie those of writing poetry, though the poet must pay infinitely closer attention to the interacting sound, texture, rhythm, history and emotional force of all the words he uses.

The present cult of functional deadness in science, industry, religion and administration, as well as in prose writing, is perhaps mankind's reflex action taken with the object of reducing itself to a more manageable size by catastrophe, and of never again attempting to think in cosmic, as opposed to terrestrial, terms. Yet when the eventual warning comes, sufficient people should still be found to enter Noah's ark, as it were, and sail beatifically away; namely, the few people who have continued to think in magical terms. One mystical Moslem view is that there are always 4,000 people around, no less, no more, however large the statistical number of births.

128

Why 4,000?—I suppose because forty is used in the East to denote any fairly large unascertainable figure, which one multiplies a hundred times for generosity. The number of true poets, painters, composers alive at a given time seems to vary little despite the increase in population. There never seem to be more of any one sort than can be counted on the fingers of a single hand. Perhaps the 4,000 include also mystics, saints, and all others who are more concerned with being than doing; which means a high proportion of women.

A friend of mine once rescued a battery hen from its battery pen and wanted to put it with free-ranging fowls to scratch for its own food; but decided that it would be at once pecked to death—so gave it in charge of a single free instructress. The bird did not at first respond to the change and many months passed before it acted in the least like a hen. Now it is managing well enough in a flock of Rhode Island Reds, and may soon be a real mother. Ordinary citizens are becoming more and more like battery hens—or battery capons—and even those who try to escape from their environment may find themselves helplessly at a loss. How to go anywhere without a car, how to go up and down flights of stairs without a lift, how to cook without electricity, how to make soup without a soup-packet, how to wash clothes without a clothes-washer, how to support life without a refrigerator, a radio and a record-machine, how to write a letter without a typewriter! Ordinary citizens use the end-products of agriculture, yet would not recognize an apricot if they saw it hanging green from a tree, or even hops if they saw them hanging from poles; or an unhusked walnut; or a tobacco flower, or a marijuana plant in blossom. Yet they are interested in space-travel and in the scarred surface of the moon, and in abstract art and computers and ocean bed exploration and in the development of plastics, and in erotic literature and psychodelic drugs

129

and electric guitars and the performances of racing cars. They have got further away from humanity and the magic of love and the simple joy of being alive than any people anywhere ever before. Being truly alive, for a poet, implies three things: affectionate understanding between friends; an intense love-life with a particular person; and the occasional luxury of being alone. To be dead is to have acquaintances, not friends; to enter on occasional sexual experiences with whoever is available, rather than to fall in love; and to hate solitude.

'A man must swallow a peck of dirt in his life-time.' But a peck is a few pounds only. Enlarged to a bushel it still remains a small amount. Most people in the Western world, however, make dirt their main diet. How many of them really enjoy their work as such? And are on affectionate, or intimate, terms with their fellow-workers? And are genuinely interested in the quality of the goods that they help to manufacture or sell, or in the services that they supply? A man may be satisfied to have made a success of his job—to have reached, for example, high executive rank in an advertising agency, where he can point to a steady rise in the sales of a particular product handled by himself, or in a new technique of sales-manship, or in the acquisition of additional accounts. But it seldom matters a row of pins to him whether the product is any better than any other of the same general sort, or whether he may be defrauding the public by asking them to pay three times the value of the product because of advertising costs. Yet it is part of his work to brainwash his underlings, especially travelling salesmen, into believing that the product *is* in fact as unique as it is valuable.

Schoolmasters beyond the most elementary teaching stages are, as a rule, discouraged from imparting any knowledge that they themselves believe strange or useful: dull and tendentious text books for their use are decided upon by central committees, against whose choice they have no recourse if they want their pupils to pass the set examinations. Although the acceptance of academic values and the power of memorizing irrelevant facts are no proof of intellectual sensibility, the students who can pass these examinations without feelings of disgust fit better into the mechanarchy than those who cannot.

In 1945 the Reverend Father Placide Tempels, a Dutch missionary, published his *La Philosophie Bantoue* at Elizabethville in the Congo. Originally written in Dutch, it has now been translated into English by the Reverend Colin King. The Bantus' reaction to European mechanarchic culture is a mixed one. They admire material inventions such as well-made tools, fabrics, medicines, motor-cars, pocket-torches, shot-guns, plastic buckets and the like, only because these promise to develop and fortify the one possession that they prize beyond all others: their vital force. Otherwise they shrink from them as diabolic. Vital force, which they call *muntu*, is in theory bequeathed them by their ancestors—as Western scientists talk of genes and inherited constitutions—and demands continuous care for its preservation. A man's *muntu* can increase of decrease according to the terms on which he lives with others: it will depend on his use of this power, for good or evil, while associating with his superiors in rank, his equals, his inferiors and foreigners; and on what returns of vital force are made. The greatest praise to a benefactor is: 'You give me life.' If envy, hatred, jealousy, insincerity or scorn are evident in another's deeds or bearing, this is regarded as a sort of witchcraft: as in the Hebrew Decalogue the command, 'thou shalt not covet', meant 'thou shalt not bewitch'. He asks: 'Are you trying to kill me?' In a native court of law, the damage to a wronged man's vital force cannot be assessed only in terms of money. The judge's task is

131

to decide who was at fault, and thereupon insist on a public avowal of guilt and a ritual cleansing. Every illness, wound, disappointment, suffering, depression, fatigue, or failure counts as a diminution of a man's vital force, and the Bantus guard against these by building-up a reserve of energy through natural magic. An autopsy on a corpse proving that a man died of an infectious illness does not nullify the relatives' plea that he died because an evil person undermined his *muntu*; in most cases the accused will plead guilty and make all ritual amends in his power.

Bantus go at times into trances and claim to be reborn with renewed magic powers; nor, like the ancient Greeks, do they undertake any creative task without appealing to a spiritual force which will enable them to dominate the material. The European traders' conversion of young Africans to the view that money will buy anything, that money alone has moral value, and that the machine-gun is a power beyond human argument, caused such a shock in many tribes that thousands of old people went into deep depression and the population noticeably dwindled. To this youthful repudiation of love, truth, and respect for tradition there could be no adequate reply but: 'My sons, you have killed us.'

European infiltration into African life has set the Bantus hopelessly at odds among themselves: a confusion increased by the often unselfseeking missionary work of rival Christian and Moslem sects. It is difficult to see how the original Bantu principles can survive, under native governments educated, administered and armed in Western fashion. Yet these are the very same principles that provide the *muntu* for Western poets who look hopefully beyond the universal mechanistic catastrophe to their restoration.

*

Shakespeare's parallel, drawn by Theseus in *A Mid-summer Night's Dream*, between the lunatic, the lover, and the poet is not fanciful if the words are all used in their purest sense.

Lovers and madmen have such seething brains
Such shaping fantasies, that apprehend
More than cool reason ever comprehends.
The Lunatic, the lover and the poet
Are of imagination all compact.
One sees more devils than vast hell can hold;
That is the madman. The lover, all as frantic,
Sees Helen's beauty in a brow of Egypt.
The poet's eye, in a fine frenzy rolling,
Doth glance from heaven to earth, from earth to heaven,

And as imagination bodies forth
The forms of things unknown, the poet's pen
Turns them to shapes and gives to airy nothings
A local habitation and a name.
Such tricks hath strong imagination
That, if it would but apprehend some joy,
It comprehends some bringer of that joy;
Or in the night, imagining some fear,
How easy is a bush supposed a bear.

Lunatic originally means someone whose emotional life is affected by phases of the moon. There are many such, not only gipsies, whose lives seem to hinge on these phases. A new moon implies holiness and promise; a full moon, intoxication of the senses; a waning moon, reflection. I myself try never to take an important decision except under a new moon. A 'lover' is one whose whole mind focuses on the object of his love, and who cannot be distracted from it by any outside influence or rational argument. The poet is lunatic in the sense that the poets' Muse is traditionally a Moon Goddess, and that

133

her love-mysteries were always celebrated under a full moon. But he is even more conscious than the lunatic of the hyperphysical influence which the moon exercises, and even more conscious than the lover of the hyperphysical influence of love.

A fellow-poet wrote on my seventieth birthday to ask whether I knew what poetry was all about; he was still in the dark. I answered that I knew a little more about it than once: such as that the problem of writing poems was like that of reconciling the solar with the lunar calendar. Every few generations or so, a full moon almost exactly coincides with the moment of the summer solstice—yet this is a phenomenon not even visually experienced. Rare and hidden correspondences between the souls of a poet and a Muse woman are what matter in poetry; they give him courage not to die while still alive, nor to fudge and cheat in any work he undertakes, nor to pity himself because the coincidence of souls cannot be prolonged or repeated. Marvell's poem makes good sense up to a point:

> My love is of a birth as rare
> As 'tis by nature strange and high:
> It was begotten by despair
> Upon impossibility.

The word *despair* seems to have been dictated by the rhyme *rare*, but even so the statement is partial. What about the woman concerned? I should have written it otherwise:

> Our love is of as pure a breed
> As 'tis by nature strange and high,
> Engendered by the lover's need
> Upon impossibility.

The subject of poetry is the certitude that, despite all

134

possible doubts and difficulties, true lovers will one day reconcile lunar with solar time, imagination with reason, intuition with planning, honour with freedom; the male with the female mind. This happens only in a timeless *now*, which must not, however, be dismissed as a fanciful *then* by its participants: it is the *now* of wisdom, the poetic *now*, the *now* of the Black Goddess—of Wisdom as Night.

As Hippolyta says, in answer to Theseus's reflections and upon lovers and madmen and poets:

> But all the story of the night told over,
> And all their minds transfigured so together
> More witnesses than fancy's images
> And grows to something of great constancy
> But, howsoever, strange and admirable.

The poet is not a schizophrene—with his mind torn in two parts—but a *deuteropotmos:* a 'second-fated' one who has, as it were, already died and conversed with the cracular dead, thus being gifted with the spirit of prophecy. At Athens anyone who had been paid funeral rites but afterwards returned alive to his family was a *deuteropotmos*, and thereafter forbidden to visit any temple of the Infernal Deities. It is active death to have been in love with a woman for ever, *meaning* for ever, and to have been afterwards betrayed, murdered and left by the wayside. And anyone who, like myself, has officially died of wounds will agree that active hyperphysical death is far more painful, and takes one far deeper down into the land of the dead than the ordinary physical sort.

THE SECOND-FATED

My stutter, my cough, my unfinished sentences,
Denote an inveterate physical reluctance
To use the metaphysical idiom.
Forgive me: what I am saying is, perhaps, this:—

155

Your accepted universe, by Jove's naked hand
Or Esmun's or Odomankoma's or Marduk's—
Choose which name jibes—formed scientifically
From whatever there was before Time was,
And begging the question of perfect consequence,
May satisfy the general run of men
(If 'run' be an apt term for patent paralytics)
That blue-prints destine all they suffer here—
But does not satisfy certain few else.

Fortune enrolled me among the second-fated
Who have read their own obituaries in *The Times*,
Have heard 'Where, death thy sting? Where, grave thy
    victory?'
Intoned with unction over their still clay,
Have seen two parallel red-ink lines drawn
Under their manic-depressive bank accounts,   .
And are therefore strictly forbidden to walk in graveyards
Lest they scandalize the sexton and his bride.

We, to be plain with you, taking advantage
Of a brief demise, visited first the Pit,
A library of shades, completed characters;
And next the silver-bright Hyperborean Queendom,
Basking under the sceptre of Guess Whom?
Where pure souls matrilineally foregather.
We were then shot through by merciful lunar shafts
Until hearts tingled, heads sang, and praises flowed;
And learned to scorn your factitious universe
Ruled by the death which we had flouted;
Acknowledging only that from the Dove's egg hatched
Before aught was, but wind—unpredictable
As our second birth would be, or our second love:
A moon-warmed world of discontinuance.

*

I have told the following story before. One fine summer

evening, at the age of twelve, I was sitting on an iron roller behind the school cricket pavilion, with nothing much in my head, when I received a sudden celestial illumination: it occurred to me that *I knew everything*. I remember letting my mind range rapidly over all its familiar subjects of knowledge; only to find that this was no foolish fancy. I *did* know everything. To be plain: though conscious of having come less than a third of the way along the path of formal education, and being weak in mathematics, shaky in French grammar, and hazy about English history, I nevertheless held the key of truth in my hand, and could use it to open any lock of any door. Mine was no religious or philosophical theory, but a simple method of looking sideways at disorderly facts so as to make perfect sense of them.

I slid down from the roller, wondering what to do with my embarrassing gift. Whom could I take into my confidence? Nobody. Even my best friends would say 'You're mad,' and either send me to Coventry or organize my general scragging, or both. It occurred to me that perhaps I had better embody the formula in a brief world-message, circulated anonymously to the leading newspapers. In that case I should have to work under the bedclothes after dark, by the light of a flash-lamp, and use the cypher I had recently perfected. But I remembered my broken torch-light bulb, and the difficulty of replacing it until the next day. No: there was no immediate hurry. I had everything securely in my head. Again I experimented; and again the doors opened smoothly. Then the school-bell rang from a distance, calling me to preparation and prayers.

Early next day I awoke to find that I still had a fairly tight grasp of my secret; but a morning's lessons intervened, and when I then locked myself into the privy, and tried to record my formula on the back of an old exercise book, my mind went too fast for my pen, and I

K   137

began to cross out—a fatal mistake—and presently crumpled up the page and pulled the chain on it. That night I tried again under the bedclothes, but the magic had evaporated and I could get no further than the introductory sentence.

My vision of truth did not recur, though I went back a couple of times to sit hopefully on the roller; and before long doubts tormented me—gloomy doubts about a great many hitherto stable concepts, such as the authenticity of the Gospels, the perfectibility of man, and the absoluteness of the Protestant moral code. All that survived was an after-glow of the bright light in my head, and the certainty that it had been no delusion. This is still with me, for I now realize that what overcame me that evening was a sudden awareness of the power of intuition, the supra-logic that cuts out all routine processes of thought and leaps straight from problem to answer. I did not in fact know everything, but became aware that in moments of real emergency the mind can weigh an infinite mass of imponderables and make immediate sense of them. This is how poems get written.

I have since found that this mystic experience is not at all an uncommon one. Something like one person in twenty has enjoyed it and I am convinced that the original moment, when Adam and Eve first looked at each other in wonder under the moon and signalled 'We are We', was an experience of the same sort, complementarily enjoyed by both: their foretaste of ultimate wisdom.

> How often have I said before
> That no soft 'if', no 'either-or',
> Can keep my obdurate male mind
> From loving true and flying blind?
>
> Which, though deranged beyond all cure
> Of temporal reason, knows for sure

That timeless magic first began
When woman bared her soul to man.

*

I have been looking at the poems of Yevgeny Yevtushenko, as translated by George Reavey. Since I cannot
read Russian which, everyone agrees, is—next to English
of course, and some say Demotic Greek—the best living
language for poems, because of its extraordinary shades
and graduations of meaning, I can judge Yevtushenko's
general attitude to poetic principles only as evidenced by
the translations. It is an attitude noticeably deformed by
a Marxist education and Yevtushenko's dependence for a
living (and indeed for avoidance of gaol) on the vagaries
of the political censorship. His preoccupation with the
perennial danger of being a Russian poet—as George
Reavey says, 'one need only mention the tragic fates
that befell Pushkin, Lermontov, Blok, Gumilev, Yesenin,
Mayekovsky, Mandelshtam and Tsvetayeva'—makes
him advance with forced assurance, very carefully *not*
looking over his shoulder. And although demanding the
freedom to be a poet and an individual he insists on his
'hard, proud faith in the Revolution' and on his hatred
of those who have betrayed it—especially of Stalin,
because Yevtushenko's poetic life began after Stalin's
death and posthumous disgrace and the stigma thereupon
attached to the personality cult. He also proclaims his
nationalistic pride in Russian space travel, and attacks
his fellow-citizens for not reaching above mediocrity in
the true spirit of the Revolution.

Here is a seemingly dangerous poem:

The twentieth century has often fooled us.
We've been squeezed in by falsehood as by taxes.
The breath of life has denuded our ideas
As quickly as it strips a dandelion.

139

As boys fall back on biting sarcasm,
So we rely for our trusty armour
On an irony not too unobtrusive,
Not too naked either.

It has served as a wall or dam
To shield us against a flood of lies,
And hands have laughed as they applauded,
And feet sniggered as they marched.

They could write about us, and we've allowed them
To make movies of this scribbled trash,
But we have reserved the right
To treat all this with quiet irony.

In our contempt we felt superior,
All this is so, but probing deeper,
Irony, instead of acting as our saviour,
You have become our murderer.

We're cautious, hypocritical in love.
Our friendships are lukewarm, not brave,
And our present seems no different from
Our past, so cunningly disguised.

Through life we scurry. In history,
Like any Faust, we've been pre-judged.
With Mephistophelian smile, irony,
Like a shadow, dogs our every step.

In vain we try to dodge the shadow,
The paths in front, behind, are blocked.
Irony, to you we've sold our soul,
Receiving no Gretchen in return.

You have buried us alive.
Bitter knowledge has made us powerless,
And our weary irony
Has turned against ourselves.

However, be not deceived! This poem is written not about himself and his contemporaries in Moscow but about the *littérateurs* of New York City; and purports to prove that he has not been fooled by the crude materialistic comforts of Capitalism. Here is another poem:

THE AMERICAN NIGHTINGALE

In the land of perlon and dacron
And of science that has become a fetish,
I suddenly heard a kindred, kindred sound—
A sound quite inimitable and pure.
A branch can easily bear a bird,
And on one of those branches
This American nightingale was perched,
Singing just like a Russian nightingale.
Mournfully he sang, and happily,
And someone stormily unleashed
Flashes of lilac clusters in reply—
This earth's awakening joy.
This was in Harvard in the spring.
There everything was topsy-turvy—
In laughing Harvard's merry-go-round,
Swaying drunkenly after the exams,
The students sang, out on a spree
And to their foundations all things
Seemed mixed in a rainbow cocktail
Of students, birds and flowers.
Proudly, unfailingly, that nightingale—
That so kindred nightingale—thundered
Above the half-truths and the lies,
Above all the restless chatter,
Above all the black deeds,
Above the millions of questionnaires
And the shark-like bodies
Waiting for rockets to spring into action.
And somewhere in the heart of Russia
The same sort of little scamp,

141

Restively opening his small beak,
His little Russian brother sang
In Tambov, Harvard, and Miami,
For the delight of villages and cities
The branches in all the gardens bent
Beneath the nightingales in ecstasy.
The music, like a blizzard, lashed
One continent and then another . . .
All nightingales will understand each other,
Everywhere they speak one language.
In their tremulous union,
They sing ever higher, more tenderly.
But we men, shall we never
Understand each other?

My contention has long been that facts are not truth,
though facts may challenge truth. To assert that the
Sheldonian Theatre lies opposite St John's College in the
Cornmarket, and to base some mystical argument on this
geographical affinity, would be untruthful. It detracts
from my pleasure in Keats's sonnet 'On First looking
into Chapman's Homer', not that Homer had been denied
to Keats in the original Greek, but that he used a metaphor of stout Cortés gazing on the Pacific Ocean, silent
upon a peak in Darien—when Pisarro's lieutenant Bal-
boa, not Cortés, was the first European to see the
Pacific. Does it matter? It does to me, because the original very humorous account of this occasion should have
fixed the name in Keats's mind: he is using secondary,
not primary, sources. So with Yevtushenko's ornithology.
It is true that the Eastern European nightingale sings as
far north as Tambov; whereas the Virginia nightingale
(it only winters in Virginia), never reaches Massachusetts, except as a cage bird. Anyhow, this Virginia
nightingale is a grosbeak, not a nightingale, as can be
observed from its entirely different plumage and song.
There are in fact *no* true American nightingales, nor do

grosbeaks and nightingales confabulate amicably. True nightingales are choosy birds: the West European variety avoids Ireland and Brittany, though visiting all other parts of France and the British Isles.

A nightingale does not naturally seek out other nightingales: its song, like the robin's, being a claim to rule a certain territory. Nor is Yevtushenko's 'Nightingales of the World Unite' cry a poetic one. Nor are poets members of a football team—Yevtushenko made a great reputation on the football field—to address as 'brothers' and urge goalwards under the coloured jerseys of Walt Whitman or Pushkin. He is puzzled by his fellow-poets, the angry young men of America, who rebel against the twentieth century, the great age of the sputnik. What they want, he says, he doesn't understand. He speaks to them bluntly, a fellow-poet just arrived from Moscow, as man to man, harbouring no wretched disbelief but loud in love for his country, battling in her ranks. *Their* eyes, he says, shine with contempt for the age, they despise political parties, governments and philosophizing seers. The twentieth century is not a father to them, but a mere stepfather.

It is true enough that most run-of-the-mill poets in America feel obliged to choose between academicism and revolt; but when Yevtushenko summons the great Twentieth Century with its triumphal sputnik to pluck them out of their dark confusions, he is speaking as a politician, not a poet. Russian academicism is the direct result of the Russian Revolution and out-academicizes any Western academicism because more carefully controlled by the Party. There can be no revolt in Russia because the Revolution was the revolt to end all revolts; and Yevtushenko does not feel entitled to criticize his country except by saying that it has not lived up to the standards it has set itself; he cannot openly quarrel with the standards.

One of his first errors was to write a poem called *Babi-Yar* about the wartime massacre by Germans, in Russia, of ninety-six thousand Jews. It made Yevtushenko suspect of accusing the Party of anti-Semitism: he had singled out the massacred Jews and it was complained that this would create the impression of their having been the sole victims of Fascist oppression. He was eventually forced, by the embarrassing interruption of his reading with enthusiastic cries of 'Babi-Yar, Babi-Yar', to insert a few lines telling how a Ukranian woman had lost her life in trying to save a Jewish child. That put him right with the Party, but it was a warning which he has ever since been obliged to regard.

The most politically dangerous side to Yevtushenko's poem-writing and dramatic readings is that it encourages a personality cult of poets—something that has always set the democratic Russians against them—a danger that a football team, or a local soviet, or an orchestra, or a *corps-de-ballet* can disregard because their leading performers are dependent on others for their success. That a poem is a single poet's work, and recognizable as his alone, has its obvious disadvantages. In theory all men should be equally talented, especially the proletariat, without any nonsense about genetics. Yet the poet cannot remain anonymous unless the poem is composed on ballad lines for communal singing among close friends and constantly added to, or altered, by these and their successors.

Yevtushenko can best be understood from a record of his recitations, which are theatrical triumphs. All the organ-stops, growls, yells, groans, whispers, sneers are used with what used to be called 'rabble-raising eloquence'. Either the listener must allow himself to be enchanted, or he must fight the enchantment; the American poet Vachel Lindsay used much the same technique; so did Dylan Thomas the Welshman.

Trained actors read poems in the style taught them by elocution teachers. Not a syllable is lost. Every word is made to tell . . . personally, I cannot stand it. I suppose because I know that the truer the poem, the more it loses from being recited in a trained voice to a large audience. As with a folk-song, or an Elizabethan love-song played on a lute, the smaller and more intimate its audience the better.

Recently in New York I recorded poems for a long-playing disc. The other four or five records I had made elsewhere sounded all wrong, as if I were reciting the poems to an auditorium of ten thousand listeners; the theatrical falseness was obvious. So now I went to the studios without a collar or tie, kicked off my shoes, called for a Scotch-and-soda, and shooed everyone out of the studio except my three closest New York friends—two painters and a composer, whom I had brought with me. I talked the poems to them in the ordinary voice I use when something really interests me, having asked them to raise a finger whenever a wrong note crept in—so that I could at once say 'Cut!' and read the poem again. The studio officials were behind glass; I paid no attention to them. As a result the poems sounded very much as they had sounded in my head while I was composing them.

The principle is important. In ancient days a group-spirit created by common interests of work, defence, kinship, habitat, and sharing of natural resources allowed one to declaim a poem to a gathering of two or three hundred people and be accepted by every heart. It may still be possible to do this in a few anthropological back-waters of Africa and Oceania. Everywhere else, except for rare cases of common disaster or danger, the natural group-spirit has disappeared, and a false one has been created as a convenience for government either by a despot or by a cult priesthood.

Such priesthoods are not necessarily religious: indeed,

145

Marxism, although patriarchal in spirit, is avowedly atheistical. And the dominant Western Mammon cult which is equally patriarchal but has tried to absorb religion in its system, wars against the Marxist priesthood with the utmost bitterness. Both have enlisted mechanarchic help to further their control of the masses and to break down all local attachments of a superstitious nature. For Marxists, what really matters in theory is that workers should work in unison for their common benefit; for the Mammonists, all that matters in theory is that the consumer should consume more and more, and the producer should produce more and more. In both cases, the priesthood, like the tribe of Levi in Israel, are financially supported by the masses, and claim rights of ideological decision denied to them. This is a closer analogy than appears at first sight: the Levite priesthood under the Alexandrian-Greek House of Boethus, which had collaborated with the Romans to keep the Palestinian Jews quiet and hard at work, contained a group of millionaires.

There is, however, a certain difference between Marxists and Mammonists in their attitude to poetry, music and the arts. Marxism has got tied up with social realism, which means that because the arch-enemy Mammon exploits the workers and grinds their faces, one must concentrate attention in art and literature exclusively on this simple phenomenon; whereas Mammon has got tied up with religion, which means that the glories of this world must be despised in favour of those promised in the world to come—so long as the producer produces whatever the consumer can be persuaded to consume, and so long as the market remains scientifically controlled. Nevertheless a producer who can sell his poetry, paintings, sculpture or music to the consumer, whatever their quality or ideology, is not discouraged. That some of these goods are not only irreligious but un-

146

scientifically produced, mostly by hand, and show a marked difference from the products of factories, makes their value a variable element which few financial experts can assess. The very rich get fun from forcing up the price of these products, and inviting the producer to their salons.

A poet is often tempted to become a 'do-gooder' by organizing political interference with the mechanarchy, rather than by giving a personal example of how to be oneself and not a conditioned human machine. He can have a certain foreknowledge of eventual miracle; and, for a poet, what will be, is.

Concentration on force of circumstances has distracted me, for the last few minutes, from talking about poetry. I should have kept off the subject of literary concerts and Marx and Mammon and dwelt, rather, on poetic love. It happens in country places, and even in towns, that a boy and his girl have never had eyes for any but each other; they court and marry and are one for the rest of their lives. It is different with poets, who fall wholeheartedly in love, suffer every agony by love's souring, find themselves alone again, catch at partial love, throw it off, and again give their whole hearts—this time, they swear, for ever. What went before was doubtless true love, and though it has been superseded in time, they still have fragrant memories of it, or a sad sense of having been at fault, and still treasure tokens of its nobility. If it had not been for these earlier loves they would not be their new, informed, wide-eyed, still innocent, still passionate selves, constantly enlarged in sensibility. And unless this is understood by both partners in a final love bond, with unjealousy shared and then viewed as growing pains of an understanding so close that it illuminates the whole world . . .

But there is no 'unless' for poets.

Circumstances oppress and threaten, but lack poetic

147

reality. Lovers should never plan, which means to consider the result if a conjectural course is taken; for conjecture has no part in love. Every practical question should be settled by instinctive action when the time comes. Talk between lovers should be signals of common awareness; with an implied blessing on all the loves that each has had before, leading to this culmination.

A LOST WORLD

'Dear love, why should you weep
  For time's remorseless way?
Though today die in sleep
  And be called yesterday,
  We love, we stay.'

'I weep for days that died
  With former love that shone
On a world true and wide
  Before this newer one
  Which yours shines on.'

'Is this world not as true
  As that one ever was
Which now has fled from you
  Like shadows from the grass
  When the clouds pass?'

'Yet for that would I weep
  Kindly, before we kiss:
Love has a faith to keep
  With past felicities
  That weep for this.'

It is usual to talk of the male and female principles as being present together with varying proportions in most people. I find this physiologically confusing, though indeed natural *baeddels* (from which Anglo-Saxon noun the adjective 'bad' is derived) are often born: effeminate

men, mannish women, cocks in hen's plumage, herma-
phrodites. It is easier to think of the situation in terms of
Sun and Moon. The Sun in the Western world has been
for some three millennia associated with man as the King,
from whom the Moon, his Queen, borrows a dim and
secretive light. The White Goddess about whom I have
so often written rules the Underworld and the Sea, but
is also a Moon Goddess; and in this context the poet has
been a Sun Hero ever since the Heroic Age. But Eastern,
and even Western, mythology also allows for love
between a Sun Goddess and a Moon hero. It may be that
the great mechanarchic catastrophe for which we are
waiting, now that all moral values and religious concepts
are being turned upside down, will involve a poetic
change from Woman as Moon—you will remember the
famous Egyptian stele of Akhenaton as the transcendental
Sun-God and Nefertiti as his Moon Goddess—to woman
as Sun. In extreme cases of poetic love, even where the
poet is Sun-like in his maleness and heroic pride, while
the Muse-woman appears to be wholly ruled by the
Moon, an interchange of planetary influences may be
observed. The incarnate Muse will borrow the poet's
Sun; the poet will borrow her Moon. When the Unicorn
(who began as a metaphor of the Sun's course through
the five 72-day Egyptian seasons) lays his horned head on
the lap of the pure Moon-Virgin, their spirits are united.
I have mentioned the impossibility of reconciling Solar
and Lunar time; yet it is mythologically recorded that
the Sun-Goddess Grainne and her lover the Moon-hero
Diarmuid bedded together every evening of the year
during their flight across Ireland.

THE BEDS OF GRAINNE AND DIARMUID

How many secret nooks in copse or glen
We sained for ever with our pure embraces,

No man shall know; though indeed master poets
Reckon one such for every eve of the year,
To sain their calendar.
                      But this much is true:
That children stumbling on our lairs by chance
In quest of hazel-nuts or whortleberries
Will recognize an impress of twin bodies
On the blue-green turf starred with diversity
Of alien flowers, and shout astonishment.
Yet should some amorous country pair, presuming
To bask in joy on any bed of ours,
Offend against the love by us exampled,
Long ivy roots will writhe up from beneath
And bitterly fetter ankle, wrist and throat.

LECTURE THREE

Lecture Three, 1965

With this lecture I complete the active duties of my five-year Professorship here. I shall never know whether the University has regretted its vote; but at least I have not regretted it. You may be unaware that the salary, once irrecoverable income tax and forced benevolences to the University Chest have been deducted at source, and my return fare from Mallorca and a term's living expenses have been paid, amounts to an impressive minus figure, each lecture costing me around £150.

I am grateful for being thus acquitted of having mercenary ends; and even more grateful for the licence to say whatever comes into my mind so long as I avoid obscenity, blasphemy or provocations to breaches of the peace. I have been responsible to each successive Vice-Chancellor alone—of whom none was ever ungentlemanly enough to utter a word of reproof.* I would always rather be a Court Fool than a Laureate.

One or two general comments. The historical study of Art enfeebles art. The historical study of Economics destroys the intimate magic of money. The historical study of Science confirms its degradation from an original Humanity, compatible with painting, poetry and medicine, into a mechanarchic process. It has suffered a series of apoplectic strokes: the first in Hellenistic times, the second stroke in the thirteenth century, the final stroke at the turn of the nineteenth. There may be a few

* 'Graves delivered a lecture on Virgil that outraged even people who didn't know anything about Virgil'—*Observer*, 6 February 1966. This comment on a 1961 lecture is not quite fair; when I submitted it to a couple of Classical dons for historical inaccuracies they gave it a clean bill of health.

starry-eyed young scientists still around who belong anachronistically to earlier human epochs; just as there are still a few starry-eyed soldiers, despite similar degradations of honourable warfare at these same turning-points.

As for the historical study of poetry—the first volume of Warton's *History of English Poetry*, based on a scribbled programme of Alexander Pope's, was published in 1774. Pope had arranged his design in 'eras', each marked by new subsections beginning 'School of . . .'. Warton's book and its successors, culminating in Court-hope's *History of English Poetry*, first published in 1895, one sinister chapter of which is headed 'Development of the Ethical School of Pope', have all but brought about the end of Poetry. There can, of course, be no real History of Poetry, as there can be no real schools of poetry; there are only occasional poets and poems, with swarms of imitators. Even the official *Lives and Letters* of individual poets, as distinct from the history of fashions in prosody, diction and subject, tell us little about poetry itself. The present dearth of poets throughout the Western World, but especially in the United States, is due in part to the notion that poetry can be the object of academic study and thus to the inclusion of even contemporary poems in University curricula.

Last year I discussed craftsmanship in poems; because poetry presupposes, at the very least, an intuitive understanding of how to control the reader's attention and direct his inner ear and inner eye along an intended route. This power of direction is a craft which can be learned only by writing. Poetry itself begins where craftsmanship ends; and while trying, last year, to persuade you just how certain well-known anthology pieces broke down in craftsmanship I observed that it was always easier to say why a poem is *no good* than why it *is good*.

I lived in a so-called war-zone in Devonshire throughout the Second World War, and spent a lot of my time looking at Red Devon cows on a country neighbour's farm; because there wasn't much else on the move except soldiers. I got the knack of judging a good milker and confirmed it on a visit to an Exeter cattle show, with an expert beside me. Not that I ever milked a cow in my life, but I had observed the sort of Red Devon that proved a good milker and learned to recognize something about the shape and gait and build that all Red Devon good milkers had in common. I put this knowledge to no commercial use; but it fascinated me. The same with soldiers. I had rented a farmhouse near Dartmouth and one day I called excitedly to my wife who was busy in the nursery: 'Darling, look, *soldiers!*' She said rather crossly: 'What do you mean *soldiers?*—they go past all the time.'

I repeated: 'Look, *soldiers!*'

I had learned in World War One to recognize real soldiers. And here real soldiers were marching past the house. A whole platoon of the first Commando Battalion —picked men from different regiments, three or four of them, I was glad to note, wearing the flash and grenade of my own regiment, the Royal Welch Fusiliers. No mistaking them. Real soldiers!

So with real poets. . . . What I have been telling you for the last five years amounts to this: that poetry—even *Beowulf*—is not a department of literature as studied in the English School, but a way of being and thinking: as it were the power of walking down a familiar corridor and suddenly disappearing through a stone wall at the end. A power given to few; and sceptically viewed by the academic intellectual mass, whose experts say in an off-hand way: 'Yes, of course, it is all done with mirrors. . . .'

In a way they are right. About a year ago my friend James Metcalfe, the sculptor, happened to be turning over the pages of a scientific book on mirrors: he wanted to find out whether the concentrated rays of sun from large curved mirrors could have been used by ancient metallurgists for fusing obdurate metals. Suddenly his eyes opened wide at a small diagram and he gasped: 'My God, it was all done with mirrors!'

'What was?' we asked.

'All these fantastically complicated Celtic mirror-back designs. About forty of them from the first century B.C. to the first century A.D. All from the British Isles except a single, rather earlier one, from Paris. Art-historians try to explain them away as an imaginative development of the acanthus motif. . . .'

He hurried off to an observatory, where he borrowed a set of small convex steel mirrors for experimental purposes, and later had a few more forged and polished. The intricate pattern on those Celtic mirror-backs, every one of which he succeeded in reproducing, proved to be interlinked images of several round mirrors set at different angles to one another, as reflected on the last of the series.

This is a close enough metaphor for Poetry. The source of light strikes the first mirror, which is that of immediate sensuous perception; the image is reflected in a second mirror, a more epicritic one: and if one accepts the view that every person has various degrees of consciousness corresponding to the Classical seven degrees of hypnosis, into which the poet's mind descends during the composition of a Muse poem, it is fair to say that the extraordinary complex patterns of such a poem are eventually derived from the first pure illumination of the poet's mirror. It is the *angle* at which the mirrors are set that determines the final result.

My own ineradicable view of poets, as opposed to dramatic or literary show artists, is that one cannot separate them from their work: a flaw in character will always reveal itself as a flaw in poetic craft. And the self-satisfaction derived from joining any society, cult or movement, whose laws they consent to adopt, will prevent them from insulating their work against the corrosion of dogma or convention—against deadness of soul. A poet need not be a rebel. . . . He must admit his place in the society into which he was born, while tacitly criticizing it by unrebellious but self-assured abstention from routine thinking or acting; and he must keep all his seven mirrors brightly polished.

What I like most about this University is the extraordinary freedom it allows anyone who does not abuse the right to be himself or herself, and think accordingly —so long as he or she reads the set books and causes no breach of the peace. I cannot think that the least blame attaches to University College for having sent Percy Bysshe Shelley down. The charge was not atheism but bad manners. Shelley had every right to be an atheist; and he had every right to send his *Necessity of Atheism* pamphlet around to bishops and others, so long as he kept Oxford out of his personal quarrel with the Church. But he had no right, once his authorship and University status became known, to treat the Master and Fellows of University College with contumacity, declining again and again to admit authorship.

I have been suspected, by some, of academic bad manners in suggesting that Virgil, Milton, and Wordsworth, despite the enormous respect still paid them by traditionalists, frequently departed from poetic principle. This accusation has never been brought home: I suppose because I took the advice given me in 1921 by Colonel T. E. Lawrence when he was a fellow of All Souls' and I an undergraduate of St John's; I used to visit his rooms almost daily. He reminded me that resounding invectives by young men against sacrosanct literary idols are always construed as jealousy or spite. The only effective way to rock their pedestals, he said, was by quoting pejorative textual and domestic details—the smaller and more particular the better—which would suggest that, though idols, they were not the sort of men whom one would invite to breakfast in one's rooms or trust with one's cat while away on holiday. By the way: I regret the desuetude which has overtaken that ancient Oxford breakfast ceremony. In my undergraduate days we felt no tension of time and routine, and came to Oxford for education by private talk, and by games—mostly by talk. Examination schools had to be respected eventually, but one learned more wisdom at College breakfast in one's rooms than on any other occasion. At St John's it is no longer allowed. As I was saying, T. E. Lawrence held that, for instance, the best way to break a general's military reputation was to observe and comment on his behaviour in the hunting field. So with Shelley and Pope: I have pointed out that neither could control his s's—which is a critical meiosis of mine.

It is commonplace of criticism to deny that a poet can exist without an audience. The word 'audience'—and a poet must always be extremely sensitive to the original meaning, or meanings, of the words he uses—implies a reading aloud. And although every poem should be suited for reading aloud, with full value given to every sound, pause and rhythmic idiosyncrasy—as prose need not be, because the *inner ear* to which poems are addressed is quasi-dormant in prose—a poem read silently in private yields far more of its magic truth than a poem read in a concert hall.

Perhaps the most startling difference between the world into which I was born and the world developed by the Welfare State, is that private living has been slowly put out of fashion by public, or pop, living. In modern pop living, everyone streams through everyone else's house without formal invitation, borrows what he needs and does not return it; and nobody seems to mind—I suppose because all property is now considered expendable, and solitude is identified with lonesomeness. The silent reading of poetry, which requires a high degree of private insulation, forms no part of pop life.

In the first quarter of this century, our half-starved under-privileged classes were fighting under the Socialist banner for freedom to enjoy a full life—released from the wicked Tory landlord and the wicked Capitalist. They won that fight, with the help of concessions forced from Parliament by their services in two World Wars; and most young English poets identified themselves with the cause. That fight need never, perhaps, be fought again. The laurels of victory are pop living and Telly land; and pop art and pop music and pop poetry; and 'Boy, you have never had it so good.'

The connection between pop art and pop poetry is a close one. In modern art-schools, one observes little lack of talent among the students, only lack of purpose. No one, or practically no one, has any fixed beliefs: except that all traditions must be broken because they hamper freedom of expression, and that what is brand-new must necessarily be good while it lasts. The whole corpus of art from Aurignacian cave-painting to Picasso is now finally 'out' (or perhaps Picasso is finally 'in' again, for non-artistic reasons—I must ask my contacts) and thrown into the trash-bucket or refuse bin. There are no standards left: standards collapsed when non-figurative expressionism helped the art dealers to impose fictitious values on whatever wares they could buy cheaply, sell dearly, and the output of which they could control. In my young days, painting standards were fixed: a trained ability to handle one's brushes competently and produce a picture that reflected visible nature. By the Forties, Nature had gone out; the inner recesses of the soul took her place. Revelations of these tended to be dull, one soul recess being very much like another—as you may also say

159

about coal-cellars—and soon a non-figurative academicism
appeared: it became unnecessary to judge between soul
recesses. To brisk things up, however, painters resorted
to shocking the public with stark sexual imagery, or
making them laugh with *trompe-l'œil* tricks and irrela-
vant juxtapositions of irrelevant objects. A further stage
was reached when psychodelic drugs provided all the
intricate patterns and convolutions of negative ecstasy,
and still another was reached when the long-standing
artistic protest against commercial art carried to a fine
point of sales-persuasion, was dropped; and everyone
said: 'Why be snobs? Commercial art has pop appeal. We
are people too. Why not use commercial techniques and
play the fool with them?'

This they did. But that all the different new movements were equally academic could be judged by the
way that students dressed. If a couple of seniors chose to
wear white canvas shoes enlivened by bright yellow soles
and heels, everyone else wore the same before the week
was out; and similarly with hair-styles, scarves and
waistcoats.

To be in the gaudy forefront of fashion, to *out-zeitgeist*
the *zeitgeist* is the pop artist's whole intent, to express
himself in terms of the latest possible movement, to
bicker with rivals and allies. Never to find out what he
really is—individualism has become a snobbery—or what
are his capacities and limitations and personal illusions;
but to throw reckless parties and excite a communal
spirit with which to identify himself. Often lonely figures
teach themselves a craft, to beat out something that
excites admiration and imitation and can be used as a
pointer for still another movement. The saddest cases
are artists who begin with a small genuine individual
craft, but, enraged by imitators, decide to start a new,
theatrical gimmicky style, instead of perfecting the
genuine one by an inclusion of all deeper or darker sides

of their nature, hitherto concealed, to the point at which it can no longer be imitated.

The same phenomenon appears among poets. W. B. Yeats, a good craftsman, who began with strong poetic principles, was later seduced into a period of grandiose literary showmanship. I find the later, strutting Senator Yeats a pathetic rather than a commanding, figure.

Poetry readings to mass audiences, as popularized in Russia, are now being imitated in the Western world. The pop poetry-reading, or 'literary concert', has even reached England, where the Albert Hall was recently hired for a performance of Beat poets, and filled by the same sort of audience that goes hysterical over the Beatles, the Rolling Stones, the Animals and other pop-singing groups.

The poems declaimed at the Albert Hall were, I am told, deliberate acts of rebellion against the rules or principles that control written verse. A great deal of their emotional force lay in the microphonic explosion of banned four-letter words to shock the Squares, and in the exploitation of 'significant sound', namely the confused tense battling noises of the street, bar and brothel. A modern pop-poet is an actor before anything else, and the character of his performances cannot possibly be conveyed in print. Even a tape-recording is inadequate; a small live manikin is needed, to posture and shout and be sold with every copy. In short, ultra-modern poetry is either trailed at the chariot-tail of art and philosophy, or becomes an accessory of pop music. Few pop-poets think beyond the immediate demand for kicks—and the wilder and less coherent the improvisation, the easier it is to put over. Much of it is written under the influence of marihuana, alias 'pot'.

I have nothing much to say against 'pot', except that, having been made illegal in nearly every country in the world, it gives the police a splendid chance of winning

161

promotion by planting packets of it on people they dislike for other reasons. It is far less harmful than hard liquor —here in England we have reached the point where, it is claimed, certified alcoholics and mental cases with an alcoholic history, outnumber regular Church communicants. In fact, doctors have so far been unable to prove that 'pot' causes either addiction or the lung cancer attributed to cigarette-smoking. Nevertheless, its sale is illegal. 'Pot' has therefore to be steered clear of, although the passing of a reefer around a group of friends is almost invariably soothing and harmonious in its effects: whereas one cannot say the same about a bottle of gin. Too often the bottle of gin is used to enhance the effects of pot-sodality—a nice Irish word, 'sodality'—and, often, more than a single bottle. Moreover, though occasionally beneficial in its effects—and I suspect that the famous pipe of peace smoked at tribal and inter-tribal meetings by North American indians was not merely leaf-tobacco but contained 'pot' or some similar weed, in addition to tobacco stalk—'pot' is not creative; in fact, it is the very opposite. A friend of mine had the curiosity once to tape-record his apparently inspired declamations during a 'pot' session after the reefer had gone around several times and the gin bottle had been emptied. Played back, they sounded almost as nonsensical as the seemingly wonderful poems that one composes in dream. He decided never to get high again.

The effects of L.S.D. and other psychodelic drugs are different. My own view is that a single 'trip'—and the hallucinogenes are not habit-forming—can under proper medical control be most informative. It provides an extraordinary interrelation of the senses of sound, colour and form; and reveals in pictorial imagery the hidden terrors and aspirations of the patient's mind. Yet psychodelic drugs should be taken not only after careful assurance of their chemical purity—which is always

162

doubtful unless they come from a licensed physician—but in a state of grace, which is a state of love; otherwise the mind may find itself left naked and lost, out of touch with native circumstances, and frequently suicidal.

An American Protestant priest decided last year to choose a group of young ordinands from a theological seminary, and divide them into two groups, for control purposes, one of these being given L.S.D. early on Good Friday, when they should be in the necessary state of grace for such an experience; and the other given merely a sugar *placebo*. The idea was that the L.S.D. group should get mystical visions, which might be denied to the others, and so understand the language of the great Christian mystics. I never heard what the results were. . . .

Although hallucinogenics are at first sight a dishonest backdoor approach to true spiritual experience, the mystical visions in all ancient religions seems to have been induced—after a preliminary physical purgation—by the use of hallucinogenetic drugs mixed with the sacred bread or drink. The same effect can also be achieved through eremetic austerity—St Antony's demons suggest that he was not always in a state of grace—or through schizophrenia caused by still undetermined natural causes. It might be reasonable in the present social and religious chaos to institute an initiatory rite for young citizens—a sort of Bar Mitzwah—as already, I understand, has become official practice in Norway, which confirms them in their civic responsibilities; but with discreet use of hallucinogenes to reinforce the message by an unforgettable experience. Yet the Sufi sages are right: though an ecstatic trance may be induced by purging the mind of all worldly preoccupations through the controlled whirling of the traditional Dervish dances, and by other quieter means, such as over-breathing, they attach no particular value to ecstasy. What matters is the

163

use made of the mind thus purged. They give more importance to active love of one's fellow-creatures then to mystical union with God—a principle anticipated by the Jewish sage Hillel, an elder contemporary of Jesus, who said that 'Thou shalt love thy neighbour as thyself' was a more important Torah text than: 'Thou shalt love the Lord thy God with all thy heart and soul and strength.'

Ecstasy, whether produced by austere religious self-discipline or by psychodelic intoxication, immobilizes the mind; the perceptive senses of eye, ear and touch take over and the spirit detachedly examines a self displayed in complex coloured images. If one is in a state of grace, which means bound by a poetic vow of love, to whoever or whatever it may be, the spirit will enter into the clarity of its destined paradise. But an ecstasy of horror awaits spirits not integrated, spirits not vowed to love, where all is pure confusion: the patient may be utterly appalled by the experience and even seem to be dying.

> What if my Cerberus, the mind, should be
> Flung to earth by the very opiate
> That frees my senses for undared adventure,
> Waving them wild-eyed past me to explore
> Limitless hells of disintegrity—
> Jumbled, undifferentiable fate
> Scrolled out beyond the utter rim of nowhere,
> Scrolled out. . . .
> who on return fail to surrender
> Their memory-trophies: random wisps of horror
> Trailed from my shins or tangled in my hair?

Therefore psychodelic initiation should be withheld, as it was at the Eleusinian Mysteries, from anyone whose life has not satisfied qualified observers after three years of scrutiny. A mushroom drug seems to have been used there; not ergot as in L.S.D.

Ecstasy's sole justification is a journey to a larger, unsuspected region of perception: from which the mind returns informed, and able to act.

> When the immense drugged universe explodes
> In a cascade of unendurable colour
> And leaves us gasping naked,
> This is no more than ecstasy of chaos:
> Hold fast, with both hands, to the royal vow
> Which alone, as we know truly, can restore
> Fragmentation into true being.

So we come to love ecstasy. At its purely physical level, one expects no more than a sense of ease, euphoria, steady affection; but when the physical attraction between lovers has reached its secondary and tertiary stages, so that ecstasy is attained by a mere interlocking of fingers, or even by sitting opposite each other in the same room, the result is a miraculous conjunction of souls, a foretaste of wisdom, a power communicable to all who become aware of this bond. Donne has written about this is his *Ecstasie*.

> Where, like a pillow on a bed,
>   A pregnant banke swel'd up, to rest
> The violets reclining head,
>   Sat we two, one another's best.
> Our hands were firmly cimented
>   With a fast balme, which thence did spring,
> Our eye-beames twisted, and did thred
>   Our eyes, upon one double string;
> So t'entergraft our hands, as yet
>   Was all the meanes to make us one,
> And pictures in our eyes to get
>   Was all our propagation.
> As 'twixt two equall Armies, Fate
>   Suspends uncertaine victorie,

Our soules, (which to advance their state,
    Were gone out,) hung 'twixt her, and mee.
And whil'st our soules negotiate there,
    Wee like sepulchrall statues lay;
All day, the same our postures were,
    And wee said nothing, all the day.
If any, so by love refin'd
    That he Soule's language understood,
And by good love were grown all mine,
    Within convenient distance stood,
He (though he knew not which soul spake,
    Because both meant, both spake the same)
Might thence a new concoction take,
    And part farre purer than he came.
This Extasie doth unperplex,
    We said, and tell us what we love,
Wee see by this, it was not sexe,
    Wee see, wee saw not what did move:
But as all severall soules containe
    Mixture of things, they know not what,
Love, these mixt soules, doth mixe againe,
    And makes both one, each this and that.
A single violet transplant,
    The strength, the colour and the size,
(All which before was poore, and scant,)
    Redoubles still, and multiplies.
When love with one another so
    Interinanimates two soules,
That abler soule, which thence doth flow,
    Defects of lonelinesse controules.
Wee then, who are this new soule, know
    Of what we are composed and made
For, th'Atomies of which we grow,
    Are soules, whom no change can invade.
But aye alas, so long, so farre
    Our bodies why doe wee forbeare?
They are ours, though they are not wee, Wee are
    The intelligences, they the spheares.
We owe them thankes, because they thus,

Did us, to us, at first convay,
Yielded their forces, sense, to us,
    Nor are drosse to us, but allay.
On man, heaven's influence workes not so,
    But that it first imprints the ayre,
Soe soule into the soule may flow,
    Though it to body first repaire.
As our blood labours to beget
    Spirits, as like soules as it can,
Because such fingers need to knit
    That subtile knot, which makes us man:
So must pure lovers' soules descend
    T'affection, and to faculties,
Which sense may reach and apprehend,
    Else a great Prince in prison lies.
To our bodies turne wee then, that so
    Weake men on love reveal'd may looke,
Love's mysteries in soules doe grow,
    But yet the body is his booke.
And if some lover, such as wee,
    Have heard this dialogue of one,
Let him still marke us, he shall see
    Small change, when we're to bodies gone.

And Rumi, the Persian poet, has reached a stranger
condition when the presence of his beloved is physically
felt despite a hundred miles separation.

Happy the moment when we are seated in the palace, thou
    and I,
With two forms and with two bodies but with one soul, thou
    and I.
The colours of the grove and the voice of the birds will bestow
    immortality.
At the time when we come into the garden, thou and I.

The stars of heaven will come to gaze upon us;
We shall show them the moon itself, thou and I.

Thou and I, single no more, shall be conjoined in ecstasy,
Felicitous and secure from foolish converse, thou and I.
All the bright-plumed birds of heaven will devour their hearts
    with envy.
There, where we laugh in such a fashion, thou and I.
This is the greatest wonder, that thou and I, seated together
    here in the same nook . . .
Are at this moment both in Irak and Khorosan, thou and I.

But, as Donne suggests, what matters is the curative
use to which the lovers put their minds and hearts that
have been purged by ecstasy.

I have not yet mentioned jealousy. Lovers assure each
other:

> I'd die for you and you for me,
> So furious is our jealousy,
> And if you doubt this to be true
> Kill me outright, lest I kill you.

Yet jealousy must not be confused with envy. To be
jealous is, originally, to be zealous: 'The Zeal of Thy
House has eaten me up.' The Biblical Lord God is a
jealous god: he is jealous, or zealous, for the righteousness
and wisdom of his people, not envious of demons and
false deities. In Spanish, *celoso* still has both senses. Both
the poet and his incarnate Muse are jealous or zealous for
the maintenance of the miraculous love they share; and
on finding that anyone has intervened to cloud that love,
either of them will grow murderously jealous for its
natural brightness. I do not deny that lovers grow jealous,
in the bad sense, of friendships from which they seem
excluded; which is an unfortunate inheritance of patri-
lineal marriage. In matrilineal societies men are not
jealous of their wives' friendships with other men of
noble character. The celebrated fourteenth-century
Moslem traveller, Ibn Batuta of Tangier, visiting the

Western Sudan was shocked to discover his host's wife, sitting unveiled on a divan in earnest talk with a male visitor, while the host, one Yandakan, sat on a carpet. Ibn Batuta asked, much scandalized: 'And are you, who have lived in Tangier and know our sacred law, content with this?'

Yandakan rebuked Ibn Batuta for his interference, explaining 'The free association of women with men is a good custom when decently carried out. Here it arouses no suspicion, our women not being like those of your country.'

Ibn Batuta, deeply offended, never visited the house again. Yandakan's people were matrilineal Berbers; a man's heirs were his sister's sons, not his own. A woman could divorce at will, and always remained undisputed mistress of her property, keeping her own camel brand. A husband was absolutely forbidden to treat his wife violently, whatever the provocation, and expected to bear humorously with all her caprices: though never tolerating the least injury or discourtesy from a man. Many of these customs still prevail among the Berbers on both sides of the Sudan; and seem curiously apt in the poet-Muse relation.

*

> But do thy worst, old Time: despite thy wrong
> My love shall in my verse ever live young.

European poets from Ennius onwards have hankered for posthumous fame; a weakness excusable at least in pre-Christian poets who, unless they belonged to some mystery religion, had no hopes of a glorious after-world. Few men can imagine the world going on without them, and most serious ones would therefore like to achieve something memorable, such as breeding a new rose, building an almost indestructible castle, beating the world's record for the quarter-mile, or founding an art museum.

The convenient belief in an afterworld can be so forced on children that it survives to comfort their old age. Unluckily the ecclesiastical Christian-Jewish heaven was 'frozen' as a dogma at a time when supreme magnificence and awe were to be found only in Eastern courts under a supreme monarchy. Angels, messengers, jewels, harpists; more jewels, more angels, more harpists. No sea, no streams, no trees, no grass, no beautiful women presiding over the mead-vat as in the Celtic heaven. Hardly a place to sigh for, even when peopled mainly by saints, apostles, virgins, prophets, martyrs—especially if one is a Republican citizen, as most Christians now are, or subject to a Queen. Not even organ music is allowed in Heaven; the organ having originally been a secular instrument—first made famous by that popular virtuoso, the Emperor Nero, and introduced into churches very late, after much righteous opposition and scandal.

When any ordinary person exclaims 'This is Heaven!', he does not mean the ecclesiastical Heaven where nothing occurs except endless harping, endless prostrations before the Throne, and endless choral singing. He means the garden Paradise of which we are given a glimpse in Genesis. All Paradises are much the same the world over, doubtless because induced by the same chemical action on the brain: a withholding of oxygen encourages the play of fantasy in coloured images. Paradise can be visited by saints who wear out their bodies through prayer and fasting; by drowning people; by schizophrenes whose corporeal chemistry is not working as it should; or by takers of hallucinogenetic drugs. I am neither a saint nor a schizophrene, but I have visited Paradise twice. First, when I officially died in battle—though I made no record of the experience apart from a fragmentary reference in a jocose early poem:

Above me on my stretcher swinging by
I saw new stars in the subterrene sky:
A Cross, a Rose in bloom, a Cage with Bars,
And a barbed arrow feathered in fine stars . . .
It was Proserpina who sent me back
Breathless, with leaping heart, along the track.

On the second occasion I had eaten the hallucinogenic
Mexican mushroom *psilocybe;* and was afterwards
startled to find that the deities in charge of the Paradise
that I visited—the appearances of which is authenticated
by Mexican legends and works of art—namely Tlalóc and
Chalciolithicue, correspond exactly with the Greek God
Dionysus and his mother Semele (another name for
Proserpine or Persephone). It seems that the ritual eating
of the Mexican mushroom had its Greek counterpart in
the eating of the divine food *ambrosia* ('not for mortals'),
and that the autumnal *Ambrosia*, sacred to Dionysus,
were sacramental feasts in which the divine flesh of the
bitter mushroom was eaten. Dionysus and Tlalóc—to
whom the toad is sacred—were both born from a flash
of lightning and their divine characteristics are identical
—the alleged eating of infant boys ascribed to both
apparently refers to the *hombrecitos* ('little men') as the
mushrooms are called in Mexico. As I ate the mushrooms I listened to the *curandera* (or priestess) singing a
long ritual in the god's honour, though Tlalóc had become 'Christos' for fear of the Church's displeasure. The
experience lasted for four and half hours, and began with
the usual lowering of temperature which gave me, as it
has given others, an illusion of going under water. If in
a state of grace, one visits Paradise; if not, one wishes
one had never been born.

THE AMBROSIA OF DIONYSUS AND SEMELE

Little slender lad, toad-headed,
For whom ages and leagues are dice to throw with,

Smile back to where entranced I wander
Gorged with your bitter flesh,
Drunk with your Virgin Mother's lullaby.

Little slender lad, lightning-engendered,
Grand master of magicians:
When pirates stole you at Icaria
Wild ivy gripped their rigging, every oar
Changed to a serpent, panthers held the poop,
A giant vine sprouted from the mast crotch
And overboard they plunged, the whey-faced crew!

Lead us with your song, tall queen of earth!
Twinned to the god, I follow comradely
Through a first rainbow-limbo, webbed in white,
Through chill Tyrrhenian grottoes, under water,
Where dolphins wallow between marble rocks,
Through sword-bright jungles, tangles of unease,
Through halls of fear ceilinged with incubi,
Through blazing treasure-chambers walled with garnet,
Through domes pillared with naked caryatids—
Then mount at last on wings into pure air,
Peering down with regal eye upon
Five-fruited orchards of Elysium,
In perfect knowledge of all knowledges.

And still she drowsily chants
From her invisible bower of stars.
Gentle her voice, her notes come linked together
In intricate golden chains paid out
Slowly across brocaded cramoisy,
Or unfold like leaves from the jade-green shoot
Of a rising bush whose blossoms are her tears . . .
O, whenever she pauses, my heart quails
Until the sound renews.

Little slender lad, little secret god,
Pledge her your faith in me
Who have ambrosia eaten and yet live.

172

I was never saved from drowning, but many of those who have been saved record that their forcible resuscitation was far more painful than the experience. The result of the lungs being filled with water is that the brain becomes deoxygenized. Sailors have a name for the drowners' paradise, from which few return to tell the tale. It is Fiddler's Green, sometimes called merely 'The Green', where they find perpetual dancing, drinking and jollity. According to the *Folk Lore Record* 1881, Cornish sailors describe it as an Isle of the Blest. Kirkby's dictionary of West Yorkshire dialect words places it 'ten miles 'tother side of Hell Square'—and I suppose this quotation reflects the difference between a sailor who drowns in a state of grace and one who drowns with a sin-laden conscience. I have written on this subject in a poem:

> Whoever has drowned and awhile entered
> The adamantine gates of afterwards,
> Stands privileged to reject heavenly joy
> (Though without disrespect for God's archangels)
> With 'never again'—no moon, no herbs, no sea,
> No singular love of women.
> True joy, believe us, is to groan and wake
> From the merrymakers' rout on Fiddler's Green,
> The lungs now emptied of salt water,
> With gradual heat returning to clammed veins
> In the first flicker of reanimation,
> Repossession of now, awareness
> Of her live hands and lips, her playful voice,
> Her smooth and wingless shoulders.

The phenomenon of Fiddler's Green should interest all atheists across the Iron Curtain who secretly envy Christian priests their power to mould people's characters by persuading them that righteous action in this world earns rewards in Heaven. To offer rewards only in this world has proved insufficient; under organized atheism the absence of any hell-fire threat puts a great burden on the police and their force of spies and stool-pigeons. Atheists ought to adopt the view that except in rare cases, such as a disintegrating explosion, a human being dies slowly by the stoppage of his heart; and that since the one eternity acceptable to the brain is the very last moment of consciousness—because the mind cannot consciously put an end to it—inevitably this same last moment, which one either dreads or longs for, is the sole endless Heaven or Hell logically conceivable. And if it be true that, on the point of death (as survivors attest) a man's past life swims before him, then the total sense of either triumph or guilt will be then recorded. Therefore, if the dying man has lived an honest, industrious and co-operative life in the best interests of his family, community and country, he will experience Heaven; if not, it will be either a Purgatory or a real Hell.

This sort of eternity has no relation to the eternity with which some poets credit their poems. Shakespeare writes:

> Devouring Time, blunt thou the lion's paws,
> And make the earth devour her own sweet brood,
> Pluck the keen teeth from the fierce tiger's jaws
> And burn the long-liv'd phoenix in her blood;
> Make glad and sorry seasons as thou fleets,
> And do whate'er thou wilt, swift-footed Time,
> To the wide world and all her fading sweets;
> But I forbid thee one most heinous crime,
> O carve not with thy hours my love's fair brow,
> Now draw no lines there with thine antique pen.
> Him in thy course untainted do allow,
> For beauty's pattern to succeeding men.
>   Yet do thy worst, old Time; despite thy wrong,
>   My love shall in my verse ever live young.

Although this is not a temporal eternity, since English

174

is unlikely to last many centuries more as a spoken language, the *Sonnets* are still very much alive. Their main defect is that they give us no clear picture of the beloved, but only of the lover.

All true poems have, I repeat, a durable quality. Durability need not be the antonym of temporality. The sole draft of a durable poem may be burned in an accidental blaze or torn up by mistake; and although the *Sonnets* happen to have survived, so also has *The Lover's Complaint*, which was bound up with them and is surely one of the least durable of minor Elizabethan poems, though written by Shakespeare. It begins:

> From off a hill whose concave womb re-worded
> A plaintive story from a sistering vale,
> My spirits t'attend this double voice accorded,
> And down I laid to list the sad tun'd tale;
> Ere long espied a fickle maid full pale,
> Tearing of papers, breaking rings atwain,
> Storming her world with sorrow's wind and rain.

I use 'durable' in the sense that one may buy a durable pair of gardening boots, or a pair of whipcord trousers, or plant a yew tree. A durable poem is like a durable picture. When one buys or is given a picture to hang in the living room, one gradually grows to dislike or despise it for some obtrusive alien quality, at first unnoticed, which at last becomes unbearable, and the picture has to be taken down. Or else it gradually fades away as a picture until one ceases to be aware of its colour or subject, and only a sudden unfaded patch on the wall-paper will recall its former existence. Or else it lives and lasts and welcomes one with the smile of a friend, and becomes a central fact of domestic life.

The qualities that make a poem durable are no mystery. If a practising poet revises the canon of his poem every few years, passages of time will help him to recognize the derivative, the over-clever, the flawed, the repetitious, the didactic, the irrelevant. Durability implies that a poem was written for the right reasons, at the right time, and in the right state of mind. I mean that a poem had been forming unprompted in his imagination; that the time came when its nucleus suddenly appeared—the nucleus that predetermines the whole; and that he then fell into a trance that gave him full control of his faculties: that he did not view the poem as literature or as a saleable commodity, but as self-illumination. The poet alone knows how far any particular poem has obeyed these creative principles; indeed, the sole limitation he can put on the rejection of old work is the awareness that no perfect poem has ever been, or ever will be, written. To suppress his whole canon would mean inviting the old-clothes-men of literature to republish the bad along with the good, the durable with the impermanent, in ignorant selections of their own.

It is an act of social politeness to make one's will, because of the family's trouble in dealing with certain sentimental relics. It is equally polite for a poet to cut his canon down to a reasonable size. If all his predecessors had shown decent testamentary politeness, the required reading-list of the Oxford English School would be wholesomely curtailed. After all, what the student should know about is the poems themselves, not movements or fashions in style.

I cannot honestly deny an interest in the survival of my poems, but this does not imply a quasi-continuance of my life. I reject the state-supported Judaeo-Christian afterworld and even the humaner paradise in which the Irish Master-poets so firmly believed that they would lend money, without interest, for repayment when debtor and borrower met again beside the heavenly mead-vat. Or did they believe? Was this perhaps merely a courteous way of giving a colleague what he could not hope to repay, while saving him from embarrassment? If I die in a state of grace, my timeless paradise will be the secret garden of the woman I love best.

At all events, cosmic science has done us the service of suggesting that time is no more than a useful terrestrial convention. Instead we are offered a time-space continuum in which the moment of miracle not only has its place but can be endlessly observed from endless points of vantage. In fact, cosmically speaking, to demand an after-life is to count on occupying two places at once in the time-space continuum—which is as greedy as plural voting.

Since we are able by miracle to forsee the future and re-create the past, even in our own lifetimes, what more can we ask? If we have lived our life amiss, and hope to do better next time, even a late repentance and renascence seem better than another try. If we have led poor miserable lives, there must always have been compensations, else we should have simply died; my own conviction is that rewards and punishments are neatly balanced in this world. My old nurse used to sing:

Count your blessings, count them one by one
And it will surprise you what the Lord hath done.

Granted, a continuous sense of gratitude at being alive, and in love, and having no grudge against practical circumstances—if only because of having obstinately avoided being enslaved by them—may imply that the dedicated poet has been constantly wounded and bruised by attempting the impossible. Will his poems then figure as durable records of blessedness, or will they do no more than convey, truthfully, the darkness of his self-deception? This seems to me a philosophical, and therefore irrelevant, question. A poet's destiny is to love.

177

A few years ago, after an emotional crisis, I wrote a poem advising myself to be content with the mild pleasures of old age and inaction:

> Into your outstretched hands come pouring
> Gifts by the cornucopiaful—
>   What else is lacking?
> Come, enjoy your Sunday
> While yet you may!
>
> Cease from unnecessary labours,
> Saunter into the green world stretching far
>   Light a long cigar,
> Come, enjoy your Sunday
> While yet you may!
>
> What more, what more? You fended off disaster
> In a long war, never acknowledging
>   Any man as master;
> Come, enjoy your Sunday
> While yet you may!
>
> Are you afraid of death? But death is nothing:
> The leaden seal set on a filled flask.
>   If it be life you ask,
> Come, enjoy your Sunday
> While yet you may!
>
> On a warm sand-dune now, sprawling at ease
> With little in mind, learn to despise the sea's
>   Unhuman restlessness:
> Come, enjoy your Sunday
> While yet you may!

But it was already another Monday morning; the Moon being insistent in her demands:

> In the last sad watches of night
> Hardly a sliver of light will remain

To edge the guilty shadow of a waned moon
That dawn must soon devour.
                              Thereafter, another
Crescent queen shall arise with power—
So wise a beauty never yet seen, say I:
A true creature of moon, though not the same
In nature, name or feature—
Her innocent eye rebuking inconstancy
As if Time itself should die and disappear.

So was it ever. 'She is here again,' I sigh.

Now there is not much more to say in prose—except
thank you, and good luck to my successor whoever he
may be—which is none of my business though I should
be happier if a poet rather than a historian of poetry were
elected, and one who knew sufficient Latin to write his,
or her, own Creweian Oration, in draft at least for correc-
tion by Classical craftsmen—because, frankly, Latin is
needed for the finer understanding of English poetry.
And—above all—I hope you will elect someone who
loves Oxford as dearly as I have done for two generations.
So, good-bye.

THE WORD 'ROMANTIC'

Lecture to Bennett College, New York, 1964

The Word 'Romantic'

'Professor Graves, are women more romantic than men?'
I had no time to answer with care and conviction; and
for want of a smart come-back, such as 'Feed that
to a computer', I gave the young reporter a tactical
'Don't know'—meaning that he had better pocket his
ball-point and note-book. For a true answer, I should have
had to differentiate between two main senses of the word
'romantic': the modern public one, probably dismissed
by my reporter as 'Arthurian hogwash'; and the ancient
mystical sense which, judging from his voice and manner,
he could not accept either.

'Romantic', in its modern sense, conjures up sentimental visions of a bare-headed knight doing homage to
a long-haired damsel beside a hedge of damask roses,
while his horse paws the turf in a verdurous background.
Yet the word once meant 'of Roman origin', and the
true Romans were the hardest-headed, most practical,
savage, unimaginative race known in ancient history.
They professed soldierly devotion to the Republic,
despising all the refinements of life which their Etruscan
and Greek subjects valued. And when they grew soft
enough to tolerate lyric poems, they preferred those
written by Virgil and others—in homosexual praise of
boys. Love of women meant little to them: wives and
slave girls were what one bought, mistresses were what
one hired. At meals, the husband sprawled on a couch;
his wife perched on the rail at his feet. Moreover, the
Romans remained infantrymen by tradition; 'knight',
believe it or not, meant 'registered businesssman' in
Imperial Rome.

In fact, the romantic vision of knight, damsel and roses has nothing Roman about it at all, but refers to a later and wholly different culture: that of medieval Spain, Sicily, northern Italy and southern France, formerly parts of the Roman Empire. Though overrun first by German barbarians and then by highly civilized Moslems, these people still spoke a corrupt sort of Latin. The Moslem invasion introduced European noblemen to a new code of chivalrous behaviour, and to a convention of poetic love between the sexes. Both were further refined when numerous European Crusaders settled in the Holy Land and struck up friendships with Saracen chieftains. The language of heraldry—the Crusaders arrived in the Holy Land with bare shields—is of Saracen origin, as the Arabic terms *gules* and *azure* suggest; and so are all European orders of knighthood whose members swear to honour women, show children mercy and relieve the oppressed. In earlier times, knights merely swore an oath of loyalty to their king or overlord. Edward III of England founded his famous Order of the Garter in exact imitation of the Islamic El-Khidr Order, which dates from A.D. 1200, a century and a half earlier.

However, because the Moslems claimed their faith to be as much an improvement on Christianity as the Christians claimed their own to be on Judaism, few Western historians have mentioned the powerful glamour cast by Islam over medieval Europe. Ask any well-informed university graduate about the origins of chivalry and he will answer that it began in the days of King Arthur—a cavalry leader who defended Britain against Saxon invaders after the Roman occupying forces had been withdrawn—and that it was propagated by William the Conqueror's Norman *jongleurs*, who found Arthurian legends in Wales and turned them into French romances.

The facts are that the Normans, not satisfied with conquering Britain, also won rich possessions in southern Europe; and that the Breton knights, who formed part of the Norman aristocracy, had their own Arthurian legends, which they brought to their new Sicilian kingdom. These legends confused the historic Arthur with an ancient Celtic hero of the Ulysses type, reputedly buried at Glastonbury. Under Moslem influence, King Arthur's fifth-century Romano-Celtic character—which can hardly have varied much from that of his semi-barbarous contemporaries—changed still further. He was taught chivalrous manners and supplied with new adventures from the Near and Middle East. The crazy, rambling quests of his Round Table knights among monsters and scorcerers are Perso-Arabic in origin. Arthur, indeed, became so popular throughout Sicily that the peasants there believe he lies buried in a cave on Mount Etna. It is this popular, Moslemized King Arthur—passing as a Christian, but innocent of any religious devotion—whom Sir Thomas Malory celebrated in the *Morte d'Arthur*, and Tennyson in his Arthurian *Idylls of the King* and whom Broadway has applauded in *Camelot*.

What bearing has all this historical rigmarole on the question: Are women more romantic than men? Well, first it must be remembered that the Arthurian romances deal almost solely with love and fighting; their political and economic background is of the sketchiest. Thus 'romantic' has come to imply a lighthearted unconcern for anything in the least practical. It also implies a belief that love is not, as the early Christians preached, a mere indulgence of carnal passion, but a private sacrament destined to last so long as the knight, though white-haired, wears his lady's scarf in his helmet and battles for her honour.

A hundred years have passed since Tennyson's *Idylls of the King* (supplementing Sir Walter Scott's *Ivanhoe*) planted this chivalrous ideal in North America, where it was encouraged as a healthy influence on youth by the less puritanical schools and colleges. While far from devotional, it implied at least a decent respect for virginity, a tenderness towards the young, sick and aged and a glowing patriotism. In this Tennysonian sense, 'romantic' can still fascinate both men and women wherever the words 'love', 'honour' and 'duty' have kept their ancient lustre. College men, in the protected and idealistic atmosphere of an old-fashioned campus, can still think of themselves as budding knights, and quite a number do. Though no horsemen, they may prove their martial worth by commitments to rebellious causes, while fair ladies contribute their admiration and concern. They also prepare themselves for the accolade of knighthood by midnight vigils at textbook-littered tables, and envisage, as the crown of their devotion, wedlock with a long-tressed, admiring damsel.

Outside the campus, however, lies economic reality. After graduation the starry-eyed knight must, in fact, serve dragons instead of fighting them, while perhaps hoping to hide the ugly truth from his lady. Yet, he need not have worried: romance, for her, was never more than a charming part played in a comedy prelude now over—a means to an end. All along, she knew well enough that moonlight and roses are short-lived, that she and her ex-knight must make the best of a dragon-ruled world. And that since they would doubtless be blessed with children, the pleasurable region of motherhood at least lay stretched out before her. So now she shows herself busy, practical, tender, with indulgent smiles for the wisps of former romance that still cling to their marriage like dream memories.

The ex-knight's Arthurian romanticism being stronger than hers—because founded on a male sense of honour (ladies swear no knightly oaths, nor are they bound to keep their promises)—it usually survives the first year of marriage. He does what he can to separate his unchivalrous business life from a devotion soon perhaps intensified by fatherly pride. But he cannot anticipate the enormous changes in her physical nature, brought about by two climactic events from which his maleness protects him, and which play hell with this sort of romanticism: motherhood and the menopause. Further, she is pitched into an unromantic neighbourhood life, a choice dictated by his business, and as a rule is obliged either to take a job herself, or stay at home and get immersed in the omnipresent TV dreamland. Their children, once a main link of affection, soon begin to inhabit a world of their own. How can knight and lady keep the enchantment alive, poor victims of machino-local wedlock?

Now she feels scared. Fearing that he may fall for someone else, she showers passionate love on him, especially during their vacations; but, though responding with vigour, he suspects that desperation has supplanted her former calm certainty.

Yes, of course! We know of cases where marriage is an eternal honeymoon and the blessed pair grow so alike that their very handwritings become identical; as do their tastes in food and books. They tell the same stories, stroke each other's hands, read each other's thoughts, and when one dies the other will follow within a week or two. But such couples are rare and belong to a way of life long obsolescent.

The tendency nowadays is to drown romanticism in a sea of realism: to treat love as a polite metaphor for physical attraction strong enough to justify a wedding—though the marriage will soon, both parties foresee, degenerate into a social convenience. The sacramental holiness of sex relations fades at an early age, and not among tenement-bred delinquents alone. What strikes me most, today, is the curious lack of courtesy that men show their

dates: after the first perfunctory gestures of cigarette-
lighting, opening doors, compliments and so on, they
relapse into boorishness. If a girl shows no immediate
urge to leap into bed, her suitor shrugs his shoulders and
tries elsewhere. And my impression is that the higher the
income level, the more cynical the sex game.

However, since the average man who wants to succeed
in business needs a home as proof of respectability, he will
marry and try to keep this part of his life as decent as
possible. The pair have a biological need of each other,
and divorce or separation is so expensive and inconveni-
ent that both take pains to avoid trouble. Any fading of
passion can, they foolishly hope, be remedied by the
study of sexological manuals which enlarge the erotic
field. Even a wife who does not make her husband the
centre of existence plays safe. She earns merit by for-
giving his unfaithfulnesses; and often takes revenge in
her own secret escapades.

But!

But there is still the second, the mystical, the richer
meaning of the word 'romantic', which Tennyson,
because of his moral obligations as Queen Victoria's Poet
Laureate, felt himself bound to slur over. For instance,
he condemns as foul and unpardonable the romantic
love shared by King Arthur's wife, Guinevere, with his
noblest knight, Sir Lancelot of the Lake.

Now, the original Arthurian legends, taken from
Brittany to southern Europe and there clothed in
Saracen dress, travelled north again as approved Court
literature. At first their ethics, under a thin veneer of
Christianity, were Saracenic—like the troubadour love
songs ('troubadour' itself comes from the Arabic, and
means a lute-player). But the sort of chivalrous love later
celebrated by the court poets of Henry VIII and Queen
Elizabeth falsified its original. The troubadours had
celebrated a miraculous, creative, healing love which

could wholly join man to woman by a lightning flash of mutual recognition; but which, as often as not, ran counter to all ecclesiastical and feudal ties.

The loves of Lancelot and Guinevere, Tristan and Iseult, were originally examples of this strange union which, despite orthodox Church doctrine, came to be recognized as spiritual—because of its salutary effect on others. Yet Sir Thomas Malory, a felonious English knight of the late fifteenth century, who recorded in his *Morte d'Arthur* that Tristan and Iseult lived together with joy at King Arthur's court, neither knew nor cared why this open adultery should have been glorified. Although the crusading King Richard Lion-Heart—by the way, the first English sovereign to use a royal coat of arms—had been a well-known troubadour, the explanatory tradition was now lost.

As I understand it, the troubadours celebrated love as an axis of semi-magical power joining man and woman. Yet, it was not a bond of similar tastes, like the ideal domestic affection that linked Philemon and Baucis, but of a difference so absolute as to be complementary. Telepathic exchange between such lovers supplies answers to questions not yet framed, or courage to brave ordeals not yet commanded, or the key word to some decision that neither can know is impending. If one of the lovers happens to be sitting in a room full of people and the other enters, a shock of wonder is felt. Their miraculous power irradiates the whole company: everyone comes to sudden life, feels generous, courageous, wise. An odd proof that this love has supernatural qualities is the far-fetched coincidences that attend it. Thus, should some woman present happen to mention that, several years ago, she lost a ring in some woods fifty miles off, a stranger may pull from his pocket one which he picked up there a week before, and ask, 'Is this it?' Coincidences happening to those already in love will be no less explicable,

189

and so frequent that they soon cease to surprise but come only as renewed assurances of their bond.

The miracle of poetic composition by a troubadour was held to prove the validity of his love—poems being regarded as divine gifts rather than triumphs of individual genius. A troubadour worshipped the lady who shared his visions, and who inspired him to write poems, as a vessel of divine wisdom; he would identify her with the Blessed Virgin. Rumi, the famous thirteenth-century Arab poet, had dared to say that whoever looked upon a truly beautiful woman saw God. And so mystical devotion to a 'Her Highness', *Son Altesse,* sustained the troubadour servant through perils and hardships when he went on crusade.

Yes: devotion to *Son Altesse!* Millions of people have seen the recent *Lawrence of Arabia* film which, though admirably photographed, presents Colonel Lawrence as a hysterical homosexual sadist who, for no better motive than self-glorification, led the Arab revolt against Turkey during World War I. The script-writer had never met Lawrence, and apparently set himself to debunk the romantic legend by a cynical disregard of historical fact. Lawrence was an Irish romantic in the pure, original sense, uncontaminated by Victorian sentimentality. At Oxford he had made troubadour poems his special study, wandered penniless around Syrian villages during vacations, and written a thesis about Crusader castles. He had also fallen in love with a woman who lived at Damascus, and afterwards wrote of her in the dedication to *Seven Pillars of Wisdom*—his account of the Arab revolt:

I loved you, so I drew these tides of men into my hands, and
    wrote my will across the sky in stars
To earn you Freedom. . . .

190

In his dedication she is addressed as 'S. A.', which has been mistaken for her initials; or those of Sheikh Achmed, a close Arab friend; or even of a country—Saudi Arabia. However, the hints he afterwards gave about the meaning of these two letters made it quite clear that they stood for *Son Altesse*. The story is profoundly tragic, because when Lawrence had ridden through the Turkish lines to visit her—

Love, the way-weary groped to your body, our brief wage ours
    for the moment . . .

—he was caught by a Turkish police battalion at Deraa, mistaken for a deserter and flogged into permanent impotence. So he lost her, and by way of knightly vengeance did not intervene when, after General Allenby's breakthrough at Gaza, his Arabs surrounded this very battalion and massacred them: 'By my order we took no prisoners.'

Lawrence, although an expert on the design of motorcycles, speedboats and fighter aircraft, also a dead shot with rifle and pistol, was romantic enough to sigh for war as waged in troubadour times. 'The Battle of Crécy—1346—was the beginning of the end,' he told me once. 'Those two primitive cannon we used against the French eventually sacrificed the most honourable element in war—hand-to-hand fighting—to the practical advantage of scientific slaughter.'

This made me wonder whether the proverb 'All's fair in love and war' had been coined on that battlefield; also, whether troubadour love was, in fact, always honourable. I once asked Lawrence whether it had ever happened, for instance, that two lovers, kept apart by rank or marriage, simulated a mystical bond as cover for mere sexual adventure. He thought not; its validity would have immediately been challenged by other men

191

and women who had experienced true love themselves. Rare cases occurred of a jealous noble killing his wife and her troubadour; but summary punishment was always exacted by his peers, who then laid the lovers in one grave. This, I find, is the theme of two English North Country ballads—*Lord Barnard and Little Musgrave* and *Lord Airlie and Matty Grove*—where a jealous husband afterwards admits that he has killed the finest couple in the land:

'A grave, a grave,' cried Lord Barnard
'To lay these lovers in—
But bury her on the upper hand,
For she came of the better kin.'

In course of time, the title *Son Altesse* was conferred by French literary men on their mistresses. But they debased the troubadour ideal by omitting its prime motive: namely, Wisdom-Through-Love—Wisdom being the Seven-Pillared House to which Lawrence refers in his dedication, and which names the book. A troubadour's licence to disregard the sexual restrictions binding on ordinary people has been adopted by leaders of contemporary French society as proof of their enlightenment and liberality. Husbands and wives, so long as they preserve discretion and keep their escapades within the social framework, are granted total freedom.

But one of them, a young married woman, complained to me the other day: 'Provision has been made for any gallantries we please. One thing alone is banned: true love. If a woman should inspire true love in another man, and feel it herself, there can be no open acknowledgement. That would ruin his career and position, as well as her husband's; and disgrace all three families concerned. I have the greatest affection for my own husband; but he is a realistic, hard-working man—almost a saint—

and cannot conceive of miracles. And I refuse to divert myself by playing clever little games of intrigue with men of my class. They would make me forfeit the power ever to love truly.

'I met a man once who, I thought, shared my obsession; but he soon proved to be an actor, offering me what he guessed I expected of him. I went away in the nick of time. But the gap in my heart remains.'

'Tell me, then, Professor Graves,' the reporter interrupts as this point, 'has your concept of romantic love—troubadour love—a chance of finding public acceptance anywhere today? Why not in America—or Sweden, where divorce is so easy—and where the love affairs of film stars, sportsmen and millionaire playboys are headline news?'

'No, Sir, none! And not because romantic love would be stamped out by the churches. But because, even if the woman concerned had never let her intuitions be warped by modern schooling, and even if her man had never lost his integrity and faith in women, how could their bond be recognized by any group of solid law-abiding citizens? Where could they expect more than knowing leers and giggles, or the cold stare of outraged respectability?'

Romantic love has been provided against by modern politics and economics: an increasing high-level control over the private lives of every citizen, disguised by promises of democratic freedom and increased cultural wealth. This trend, though it strengthens marriage as an institution, weakens its ethical principles—based on a vow of eternal love, which most people now regard as a dangerous fantasy.

Resolute romantic lovers may still escape from the urban rat race to the countryside or to primitive villages abroad, and there survive somehow until their money runs out and they are sucked back again. But such lovers resemble lions caught as cubs and raised in a zoo: which

193

cannot fend for themselves if freed in their native bush, and are shunned by their wild relatives because they smell wrong. It is not possible to adapt a way of thinking that originated in an aristocratic culture to a technological democratic one, however earnest the attempt.

Granted, an occasional woman who has been blessed in childhood with mystical premonitions of love's ineffable power will realize that the divine flame still burns fiercely in her. But, she asks, where is the troubadour, the knight, her male complement? There was only one Colonel Lawrence, who died thirty years ago and whose story has been almost universally misread. Ah, if only he could rise from his grave and fill the cruel void!

But the question still remains unanswered. . . . Yes, I think that women *are* more romantic than men. In the sense of their secretly nursing a concept of divine love which, perhaps in a generation or two, if the present unrealistic views of marriage have altered by then, may gain favour. Yet the chivalrous movement must begin with men, and that is for their mothers and elder sisters (I suddenly remember my very romantic, very Irish, sister Molly, twelve years older than I was) to impress on them in childhood. It may even have begun somewhere already.

Dry your tears, Guinevere and Iseult! Here's a poem, dating from before the Battle of Crécy, to put under your pillow on St Agnes' Eve—a charm for bringing the longed-for knight into your dreams with his visor up and a face that you can recognize:

SON ALTESSE

Alone, you are no more than many another
Gay-hearted, greedy, passionate noblewoman;
And I, alone, no more than a slow-witted
Passionate, credulous knight, though skilled in fight.

194

Then if I hail you as my Blessed Virgin
This is no flattery, nor does it endow you
With private magics which, when I am gone,
May flatter rogues or drunken renegades.

Name me your single, proud, whole-hearted champion
Whose feats no man alive will overpass;
But they must reverence you as I do; only
Conjoined in fame can we grow legendary.

Should I ride home, vainglorious after battle,
With droves of prisoners and huge heaps of spoil,
Make me dismount a half-mile from your door;
To walk barefoot in dust, as a knight must.

Yet never greet me carelessly or idly,
Nor use the teasing manners learned at Court,
Lest I be butchered in some distant pass—
And you pent up in some black nunnery.